I'll Get Right Back to You
& Other Annoyances

*The things that can screw up your day...
and even your life!*

I'll Get Right Back to You
&
Other
Annoyances

The things that can screw up your day...
and even your life!

CHARLES RUBIN

NEW
CENTURY
PUBLISHERS
Sonoma County, California

Library of Congress-in-publishing Data

Rubin, Charles
I'll Get Right Back to You and Other Annoyances/humor
Charles Rubin
1st Edition
Library of Congress Control Number 2010923589
ISBN: 978-0-9679790-9-0

Cover Design: Izumi Motai

Printed in the United States of America
1st Edition
12345678910

NewCentury Publishers
PO Box 750265
Petaluma, CA 94975
Tel: 707 769 9808
Fax:707 769 9779
Email: NewCentpub.com
www.NewCenturyPublishers.com
Distributed by SBC Distributors/Gardena, CA.

To my son, Michael, with
love and admiration

Acknowledgements

Special thanks to Judith Duryea, a Montana writer who sent me on a new and far better direction with this book than the one I was following. Izumi Motai, master graphics and book designer, who has been a great collaborator. Verna Shaheen for her editorial skills, kindness, and support. Elizabeth Cupp, an holistic magician, whose incredible joy, energy, laughter, and support always boost me. Gabriel Wilmoth of SCB Distributors for helping me throughout the post-production of this book (which is when the real work begins). Kazumi Nishio, the dynamic Samurai psychologist and unsung comedienne whose wisdom keeps me sane. Star Dewar, photographer, for her magic with the camera. Ryan Costello and Wendy Morelli whose laugh gauges were ones I depended on when reviewing chapters with then. Kathy Brown at Sheridan Books—thanks for always speeding things up, printing-wise. Lisa Hemingway for helping me with research. Daughter Pam for enthusiastically approving. Son-in-law Grainger Brown for being a great audience. Writers Chris Impey, Jonah Raskin, Bonnie Estridge, Elinor Stutz, and Television anchor, Tonya Mock, for providing generous quotes. My bank manager, Mallory Rodriquez, for her story (see page 188). And Doug Mason, my pal, who never stopped nagging: "Are you writing? Are you writing?"

IF YOU LIVE ON THIS PLANET, THIS BOOK HAS HAPPENED TO YOU.

I'll Get Right Back to You and Other Annoyances is a candid, comical, often poignant, often chilling, look at some of the absurdities you face daily.

For example, there's the doctor who insists your agonizing pain is a figment of your imagination, and there's the best friend who asks your honest opinion about something…and then never talks to you again after you've given it. And as a backdrop, there's a cacophony of tuneless, groaning, moaning, screeching —otherwise known as today's pop music.

Charles Rubin takes everyday irritations and infuses them with hilarity. You will identify with them, laugh at them, think about them, cringe at them, and maybe even *do something about them!*

There are those family dynamics that cruelly brand you a "nobody" unless you are a "somebody" (annoying). And restaurant kitchens where you can't see what they may be doing to your food once you've complained about it and sent it back (very annoying). And the waiter who flirts with your date, not to mention *the date who flirts back* (beyond annoying).

Much of this annoyance derives from the author's own personal experience as well as that of the people he has interviewed. So sit back, read, enjoy, and laugh. You'll live longer.

Annoyances

1

People for whom everything is always "great, fantastic, and wonderful".

Don't you want to kill them? Those positive, glowing, smiley, cheerful people that never seem to suffer any of the hardships the rest of us suffer? They ask you how you are, although you know they haven't asked that idiotic question really wanting to know.

Should you make the mistake of asking how they are, they will appear euphoric as they go into rapture after rapture about everything being "great, wonderful, fantastic".

They will tell you about the summer house they plan to build on Nantucket in the spring, and their extraorrrrrrrdinary children who are doing so welllllllll in school, and would you believe their luck? They just inherited seventeen million dollars.

Can all this be true? Can anyone on this earth be so blatantly blessed, have such good luck, amazing jobs, families to die for, no worries, and a plethora of gifts to kill for from above landing in their laps time and time again?

You sincerely, and with more than a hint of malice, hope not.

All that good fortune isn't something you want to hear if you just lost your job and all your money in the stock market and your wife is a serious shopaholic.

If anything, you want to hear that this beaming happi-ac, (who is oblivious of the fact that you have been contemplating suicide because of your problems) was a recent carjacking victim and had to spend two days locked in the trunk of a car without food or water before someone came to his or her rescue.

Or, if not anything as serious as that, something, anything, that won't make your life seem like such a total failure in comparison. Because there is no way in hell, no matter how falsely joyous the expression on your face while hearing the good news, that you wouldn't, at that moment, like to see that person fall off a cliff.

But, for the sake of argument, what if you suspect this person, who claims to have life so beautifully handled, may be stretching the truth, you have to ask yourself the following question: What are you covering up when someone inquires as to your state of existence?

Do you automatically answer "fine" without even thinking about it? Or do you own up to how things really are?

Recently, I was feeling damned depressed and just as I was being asked how I was, I found that the word "fine" was struggling, fighting even, to come out of my mouth and that it couldn't quite make it.

"Well, to tell you the truth," I finally said, "I'm feeling like crap. I woke up this morning with a terrible headache that won't quit, and my back is killing me along with my sinuses. You know, I just can't take this weather and have been advised to move to a dryer climate, but who has the money to just pick up and move? I have two kids in college and a mortgage you wouldn't believe. On top of that, my company has announced that it is decreasing all salaries by fifteen percent starting next month. I need that like I need a hole in the head. My daily goal now is to put food on the table, and have you noticed food prices recently? Who can afford to eat anymore?"

Beware. This line of conversation hardly ever penetrates the frontal lobes of the eternal optimist who is usually too self-centered to even notice you are on earth. His or her eyes glaze over, and then he or she says something like: "This too shall pass."

Or worse: "Well, I have to run. Have a nice day."

Or much worse: "I'd love to hear all your news but we're having the President of the United States and his wife and the Bill Cosbys and the Regis Philbins and Barbara Walters for dinner. Then we're off to the Bahamas for the weekend."

Any way you cut it, you are not going to come out of this conversation intact, so when you see the luckiest person in the world coming your way, duck into a doorway.

And just hide there until luckiest person in the world passes by.

2

Waking up in the middle of a colonoscopy and being told the pain is in your head, not up your...

You think this doesn't happen? It does. All too often. Waking up in the middle of a medical procedure is as unwanted a hospital experience as getting a staph infection.

This happened to a friend of mine, James Forrestal Brown who, when undergoing an endoscopic (tube down the throat) procedure, was suddenly awake and aware of what was going on.

James, a hulking ex-Marine and understandably pissed off, confronted the gastroenterologist who claimed that there was no way that he could have been awake and aware, and that he'd imagined it.

"Oh yeah?" James growled, "so I didn't wake up and hear you talking about some hooker you picked up in New Orleans? Or how you'd totaled the new Corvette you'd just bought? And how you almost couldn't make it here for the procedure today because of a hangover?"

Some doctors resort to blaming the patient for anything and everything that might go wrong during a procedure. Even when the patient dies.

"Well, he simply should not have died," you will

hear a doctor explaining to a dead man's grieving family.

Then comes the rationale. "Your husband died, Mrs. Farnum, because of an unforeseen complication. He should not have died of an unforeseen complication." Or: "Your mother reacted to the medication. She should not have reacted to the medication."

Botch jobs happen every day, probably by the hundreds. Especially when it comes to major operations. Remember the diabetic man who was in the hospital to have his right leg amputated, only to find they had taken off the left one? It was in all the newspapers at the time.

This was obviously the patient's fault. He didn't notice they were preparing the wrong leg for amputation? He couldn't say something?

Not long ago, I had a hernia operation. The surgeon told me that I would recover completely within two weeks. Two months later, I hadn't recovered and was in a great deal of pain.

Going back to see the surgeon, he offered to give me an injection that he said would give me some relief, and for four days afterwards, I was pain-free. But then the pain returned, big-time.

So there was another visit to the surgeon who told me that the reason he'd given me the injection (an anesthetic as it turned out) was so that he could determine whether or not this pain I was having was in my head and not my groin. Huh?

This was a classic case of adding insult to injury. So I was imagining the whole thing?

I realized the surgeon was trying to pin the rap on me. Which is something an irresponsible doctor might pull on a woman, rather than a man.

Where do you think the word hysterectomy comes from? The "hyster" part comes from hysterical. Women who have had trouble around the time of their periods have been thought to be suffering from some sort of depression. The common belief was that these women were said to be mentally, emotionally, and physically manifesting their ailments.

Over a hundred years ago, Charlotte Perkins wrote "The Yellow Wallpaper," a treatise on her own illness which was labeled "imagined" and "hysterical".

But men, apparently, can become hysterical, too. At least that's what my surgeon indicated.

I eventually found out that this surgeon had done the procedure in a completely different manner than the way we'd discussed and the way I had agreed.

Instead of doing it laparoscopically which involves an incision in the belly button, he'd performed it in the conventional way which means an incision on the side, cutting into additional muscle, veins, and tissue.

With a laparoscopic procedure, a patient usually recovers in a few weeks. The conventional approach can take up to a year.

This was information I got from a surgeon to whom I'd gone for a second opinion. He took one look at the site where I'd been operated and informed me that the operation had not been done laparoscopically but conventionally. I was so shocked, I almost fell off the examining table!

And that's when it hit me. The original surgeon had initially told me that the healing would take two weeks knowing he hadn't done the operation laparoscopically.

A hernia operation gone awry is one of the main medical procedures most complained about. There are actually hernia lawyers who go after the surgeons for compensation. Are all these patients imagining the pain?

I was lucky to simply escape with a lot of discomfort. Other patients die. Seemingly uncomplicated procedures and operations can take lives just as can complicated ones.

Someone with whom I worked, a very fine and likeable art director named Boyd, aged forty-eight, went into the hospital for a minor ailment. While undergoing the operation, a major artery was cut and he bled to death.

Scary, huh? There are thousands of these cases, many of which are covered up, and many of which are brought to court.

But it isn't just a case of doctors killing patients. There are also patients who kill doctors.

I refer to a friend, Dr. Michael Tavis, a well-known plastic surgeon. Mike and I were having lunch one day and the subject came up regarding disgruntled patients.

"I've been pretty lucky," Mike said. "So far, no one has come in and shot me."

Two weeks later a woman came to his office and did just that. One bullet in the heart, and Mike was dead. The woman clearly did not like the new face Mike had created for her.

The incidence of this kind of thing happening is rare. You don't hear about patients slaying their doctors very often, but you do hear, all too often, of patients dying under the care of a doctor or surgeon.

This is not to indict all doctors of being neglectful or uncaring. To the contrary, my doctor, Jill Edison, learning that I was having chest pains, immediately sprang into action. She called my cardiologist who insisted my treadmill test and my scan results were excellent and that there was no need to carry this further.

Jill disagreed, forcing the cardiologist to get me

into the hospital immediately for an angiogram. And sure enough, there it was: one blocked artery which might have killed me, had it not been for Jill.

Having to worry about fatal consequences when undergoing an operation or procedure is an enormous burden. Aren't there enough causes for death to be concerned about such as being eaten alive by a shark or a grizzly, having a coconut split your skull in two as you sit sunning under a palm tree in Bora Bora, or drinking the tea to which your wife has added a pinch of sugar and a pinch of cyanide?

You really don't need a doctor who tries to convince you that your pain is due to a rather fertile imagination, even if you did see, with your very own eyes, those elephants climbing in your bedroom window last night.

3

Friends who only listen to one side of the story when a couple is divorcing.

Long before my first wife, Genevieve, and I broke up and decided to divorce, I was getting the cold shoulder from some of our dearest friends.

The thing was, some of our dearest friends had been some of my own personal, dearest friends before I even met Genevieve. These were people I'd grown up with, gone to school with, been in the Marine Corps with, and had been close associates in the advertising business with.

It was as if Genevieve wasn't satisfied in just having her own circle of friends hate me, but she had to grab my gang too.

And if I was being treated poorly by my friends, you can imagine what being treated poorly by her friends was like. There they would be, in my house, eating my food, drinking my alcohol, using my electricity, using my toilet paper, sitting on my couch, snarling at me and darting poisonous looks in my direction that were nothing short of pure undiluted dislike, disapproval and disgust.

When it was more than usually obvious how much they despised me, I might ask them if anything was wrong, and then find myself facing their retreating backs.

"Wait a minute," I remember catching up to Debbie Wasserman who'd been a big fan of mine at one time, someone who had been extremely loving and supportive. "You seem annoyed with me, Debbie. Did I do something to offend you? Please, tell me, what is the problem?"

"I'll tell you what the problem is," she replied, her eyebrows raised so high that they reached her hairline. "I'll tell you what the problem is."

"So tell me already," I said, noting how red her face had become and how furious she looked.

"You," she sputtered. "You are the problem!" And with that, she was out the door.

I was very naive about all this and didn't catch on at first. I didn't even suspect that Genevieve was behind it. I had no idea that all these people were acting this way because Genevieve had said a bunch of stuff about me to make them hate me. I just assumed they hated me for myself.

There was absolutely no indication that Genevieve had been verbally assassinating me, gaining allies against me because, while she was doing this, she was acting like the sweet, little, devoted wife.

Then came an event in our lives that meant we were going to be living apart. But it's not what you might think. We were then residents of Old Greenwich, Connecticut, and I was commuting to and from Manhattan each day. The commute was tedious and my work in the city was unrewarding. I started a search for something better, and it didn't have to be in New York.

The "something" that came along was the offer of a great job as the creative director in a Boston advertising agency.

Genevieve and I talked it over and decided that

this was an opportunity too good to pass up. We made a plan. I would take the job, find the right house in Boston for us to move into, find the right school for our kids to attend, and when all this was accomplished, my wonderful family would join me.

Until they did join me, I would work in Boston during the week and return to Old Greenwich on Fridays and spend weekends. On Sunday evenings, I would return to Boston to begin the new work week.

On one particular Sunday evening, we were dining with friends, Jill and Mel Blitzstein, just prior to my departure for Boston. After dinner, they drove me to the train station where Genevieve said in the sweetest way: "Goodbye darling, I can't wait to see you on Friday. Take good care of yourself. I love you very, very, very, very much." The mmmmmmmmmmmMAH of her kiss stayed with me practically all the way to Boston.

A couple of years later, this same couple, Jill and Mel Blitzstein, having been severely burned when lending Genevieve $5,000 and finding they would never get it back, decided that, seeing as they'd been wronged, maybe I had also been wronged, and that perhaps I wasn't such a bad person, after all.

It was then that I learned what else Genevieve had said to them that evening after we'd had dinner and I'd run for the train:

Her exact words, according to the Blitzsteins, were: "That idiot. If he thinks I'm really moving to Boston, he is out of his mind…"

It was only through the many, many other people who'd been burned by her, usually financially, that I eventually heard more and more of what she'd said about me. In fact, there came a time when people were practically lining up to tell me what had been bandied about between them.

Apparently, Genevieve had branded me as dull, boring, abusive, evil, bad in bed, neglectful of the children, a creep, a devil worshiper, vicious, miserable to be around, a loudmouth, cheap, stupid, an oaf, crazy, a liar, self-centered, an alcoholic, a drug abuser, a neat freak, a control freak…

This was outrageous! A completely fabricated exaggeration! I like to joke that I was only half those things!

At any rate, I could now, hearing all these stories, understand why people considered me a monster.

And I could also understand why there had been a chorus of cheers all around when Genevieve pulled a "Godfather" stunt on me.

This memorable event began one Friday evening. I'd just returned home to Old Greenwich from Boston. I was very surprised when Genevieve greeted me at the door with a kiss on the lips. What was going on? She hadn't come near me in months. She'd moved out of our bedroom into a guest bedroom, citing how she didn't want to bother me with her snoring.

She had also, as I discovered, deposited her wedding ring in a little ceramic jar on the dresser, never again to be worn by her.

But here she was that evening, looking gorgeous. She'd even made a gourmet dinner for just the two of us. Where she had stashed the kids, I didn't know. They, by the way, also seemed to hate me.

After dinner, with candlelight and wine, we sat and reminisced about so many things, fond memories, and how grateful she was for the way I worked so hard to give her and the children a good life and how devoted to her and the children I was, and then she walked me up the stairs to my room, kissing me goodnight at the door saying "I'll see you in the morning, darling."

"Aren't you going to come in?" I asked, assuming that's what the evening was leading up to.

"Not tonight, dearest," she said coquettishly, "I want you to get a good night's rest".

In my room, I was so excited, I could hardly sleep. I considered this change in Genevieve to be the beginning of a whole new chapter for us. We would recreate the happiness we once knew. I was sure that some kind of miracle had taken place.

The first thing I heard the next morning was my name being called. It was Genevieve calling sweetly from downstairs, telling me there was someone to see me.

Someone to see me??? Glancing at the clock, I saw it was 6 a.m. And it was Saturday. Who would be in my house wanting to see me at that hour on a Saturday?

I threw on a bathrobe, and as I came down the stairs, I saw a man in a trench coat standing there. I didn't know him, but registered that he looked, with his short top and sides and polished shoes, like the kind of movie hit men who were so meticulous about their appearances.

"Can I help you?" I asked, waiting for him to pull out a gun with a silencer.

Instead, he pulled out some kind of document. Without saying anything, he walked over and tried to hand it to me. I didn't know what it was and didn't take it. He just tapped my shoulder with it, and it fell to the floor.

"You've been served," he said.

I looked at him in astonishment. Who was he? What was that official-looking document on the floor?

"Have a good day," he said as he walked to the front door and out.

The document turned out to be a notification that I was to vacate the house and that I had two weeks in which to do it. After I finished reading it, and was still in shock, I started to ask Genevieve about it. But she wasn't there. She had gone into her room and had closed the door. Our life together was over.

This episode of marital demise reminded me of the scene in the movie, "The Godfather", when a man (apparently a stoolie) is taken out to dinner by the mob and treated like royalty. Then after dinner, he is garroted to death.

I didn't see much of Genevieve and kids during those last two weeks. They piled into the car and took off to stay with friends in Vermont. They even took the dog, a black lab whom I'd named Pops Von Woof Rubin. Pops had been my only ally.

From what I understand of situations like this when one spouse denigrates another, those who are sold a bill of goods are often willing to support the person going public.

The other spouse probably won't, for the longest time, even know, that which is said about him or her. There will be no hearing, no trial, no compassion. But there will be the condemnation.

So now, when I'm approached by someone complaining about a wife or husband, I think how easy it is to fall into that trap where I could so willingly be siding with that person ripping his or her spouse to shreds.

I view this as extremely unfair to the partner who is not there to argue his or her case. Instead of seeing this as one terrible partner who does all the dirty deeds and one great partner who is the suffering martyr, I see them equally taking part in the disintegration of their marriage.

And then I automatically side with the husband.

4

Enough about sex already.

When my son, John, was about twelve years old, he overheard some people talking about oral sex and came up with his own explanation of that pastime. In his still innocent way, he informed me that he knew what oral sex was.

"It's when people talk about it."

Judging by the way so many people rabbit on about it, John was right.

Frankly, I am not interested hearing people talk about their coupling habits. This has nothing to do with prudishness. This has to do with wanting to preserve how we used to think of sex in the good old days:

Nasty, dirty, and PRIVATE.

It was forbidden, taboo, sinful, vulgar, smutty, coarse, lewd, filthy, and licentious.

And delicious.

I want us to go back to the time before people weren't being destroyed by sexual scandal, when the proclivities of American presidents weren't in the headlines, and when the King of England would abdicate over it.

All the current discussing, analyzing, dissecting, mulling over, pulling apart, delving into, and intellectualizing is ruining it.

Worse, we are taking the mystery out of it.

I don't want you to tell me if you are an adulterer, a nymphomaniac, a child molester, gay or straight. That ruins all the fun in my speculating as to what you are. How can I gossip about it with friends over coffee if all your information is out in the open?

The less I know, the more tantalizing.

In movies, I don't want to see the act carried out by carefully draped actors gyrating up and down, up and down, up and down on squeaky bed springs with all the accompanying moans and groans.

I've lived in enough apartments with enough squeaky bed spring noises coming from the apartment above to last a lifetime. I'm quite aware of what goes on, thank you.

And just try getting through the checkout line at the supermarket without being besieged by the multitude of magazines that offer, in great detail, all the information on great sex.

Personally, I prefer to try the 57 positions that are vaunted in the steamy pages of a magazine rather than to read about them. And for all those tips on how to have an incredible orgasm? Reading isn't the same as experiencing.

Even a picture of deep throat kissing can be repulsive if you look at it objectively. All those movies, with the characters in close-up, their tongues going like propeller blades, ugh...it's a turn off. Unless, in my private life, one of those tongues is mine.

Just, for a moment, consider this: A man enters a room. He sees his love in a far corner. He rushes to her. She rushes to him. They're like refrigerator magnets meeting at the mouth. They stay connected this way for a full minute. Say you were a Martian who had just landed on earth and you saw these two people. Wouldn't you wonder about it?

It's like other things we see everyday and take for granted. Such as women's high heels. Our friend, the Martian, is now completely puzzled. Why would an earth woman want to walk around with a spike coming out of her heel?

The answer again, has to do with sex. Women cripple themselves by wearing such contraptions as high heels because the style attracts guys. No matter what shape a woman's legs—skinny, short, fat, shapeless, bowed—high heels make them look a thousand times better. What's more, by wearing them, women don't have to say anything. Their feet do all the talking.

Come to think of it, maybe that's a good thing. Because another turnoff is the partner who talks about sex while you're having sex. Why do people have to yak about it in the sack?

And how about the Judge Judy or judge Jim of the bedroom? The lover who rates your every performance on a scale from one to ten. Quickest way to lose interest is to have the person you're with taking notes.

As for secrecy, there's a lot to be said for it. In this day of sexual enlightenment, everyone has to have a sexual label. It's worn in the same way people wear the Gap, Banana Republic, Saks Fifth Avenue, and Footlocker labels. It's more information than is needed.

But back to my favorite thing about sex, the innuendo. We need to revive it. We have to return to the time when all that whispering and the spreading of malicious gossip was a source of intense pleasure.

Let's also bring back unconfirmed scandal; the kind of thing where nothing is proven, just speculated upon year after year. To get that whole movement going, let's take the leagues of elderly spinsters out of retirement so that they can peek out from behind lace curtains to spy on adulterous neighbors.

An elderly neighbor of mine qualifies as the Miss Marple of the sex scandal world. There she goes, telling me about one such person, a woman of about forty who circumspectly enters a nearby park at exactly noon on Thursdays, only to be followed a few minutes later by an equally circumspect gentleman.

"Maybe she goes there to play cards with him or something," I suggest.

"On her back?"

"How do you know she was on her back?"

"Just look at the grass on the back of her coat when she leaves."

This is the kind of grist that makes for a very interesting mill.

And one final thing I wish would change. Women who behave just as gross as the guys. Apparently, when they get together with their girlfriends, their line of gab would shock any man overhearing it.

These gals even have dildoes. They sit around and compare notes on their joy toys, where they got them, how much they cost, what size they are...

What's left for a man to offer? In the old days, when people had sex, the music would swell and the oceans would roar. Nowadays, the only thing that roars is Ms. Motor Mouth giving you directions on how to find her G-spot.

And if you're a sensitive guy who wants to get to know a woman before going to bed with her, you're considered weird or gay or both.

It would be nice if the whole subject of sex could be put on the back burner for a while. This would give us all a chance to talk about something else for a change.

God knows, there are thousands of other subjects. There's...

And then there's…
And how about…

5

People who act like your ideas are useless...and then steal them.

I spent a great part of my life as a copywriter and later, as a creative director in the ad business. If there's one place where you have to watch your back it's in the ad business.

Especially with the people you trust the most.

One of the supposed signs of true friendship is the candid reply. You ask your friend what he or she thinks of something you've done, some idea you've had, some creative endeavor, and they tell you honestly whether there's any merit in continuing with the project.

I had this art director I worked with—let's just call him Nat Belladoni. He was a graphic genius, but he had no aptitude for concept. We would be assigned to do a series of ads, and he would just sit there and wait for me to come up with the ideas.

Then he had the audacity to criticize them!

It didn't bother me especially because Nat would make my concepts look absolutely stunning. He knew layout, he knew type, he had exquisite taste.

One night, we were riding the subway together on our way home (he lived in the same neighborhood) in Manhattan, and I suddenly had an idea for a subway poster.

"For Christ's sake, give," I said.

"What are you talking about?" Nat replied.

"For Christ's sake, give," I repeated. "I just thought of a poster idea for the Catholic Charities of New York."

"Nah, I don't like it," Nat said.

"Well, I do, and you're going to do the layout and we're gonna sell it to the Catholic Church."

"You're outta your mind. They'll never buy anything like that. Anyway, I think it stinks."

"Just lay it out, and I'll sell it."

A week or two later, I made an appointment with the Catholic Diocese of the City of New York, located in the St. Patrick's Cathedral Church Administrative Offices on Madison Avenue. And sure enough, Nat was right. They wouldn't buy it. The nuns working in their Public Relations office loved it, but the Father in charge of advertising? Definitely not.

"See," Nat said. "I tolja they wouldn't buy that piece of crap."

"Yeah, " I said, "but the Protestants will…" And they did. The poster appeared on the New York subway system and was a great success. It was as if people couldn't wait to pour money into this charitable organization.

Not only that, but the poster won a number of awards—Clio, Addy, AIGA, etc. With Nat listed as the art director, which he clearly was not because I had even suggested the type face and the layout: Reversed Franklin Gothic on a black background.

Nat was only the "wrist" (a derogatory ad label for someone without a brain in his head, just someone who does exactly what you tell him).

But I liked Nat. In fact, I once saved his ass when he was about to be fired from the agency, his lack of conceptual skills being the reason. He did eventually leave the agency when he landed a job where he could be a full-time wrist and not have to worry about all that concept stuff.

After a few far-spread lunches with Nat, we lost touch. I went on to leave the country and to settle down in England for quite a long time. I returned with my family after twelve years and bought a house in Old Greenwich, Connecticut.

One day, while browsing in a secondhand bookstore, I was leafing through an old copy of Communications Arts Magazine that had been issued the year I went to live in England, and there it was: my poster for the Protestant charities. I had no idea the magazine had chosen my poster for top honors that particular year.

Looking at the credits, my eyes almost fell out of my head. They were as follows:

Concept: Nat Belladoni
Design: Nat Belladoni
Copy: Nat Belladoni

I have no idea whatever happened to Nat. I can only imagine he is retired. Or maybe dead. He wasn't the first person I'd worked with who'd ripped me off. Nor was he the last.

But I learned a lesson from this episode: there's only one thing worse than the person who praises your work, and then steals it...

...And that's the person who rejects your work... and then steals it.

6

People who ask you to leave your name and number on their voicemail so they can get back to you.

And then never do.

In the grand scheme of things, this lie doesn't rank with the greatest ones ever told, but probably holds the record for perhaps the most frequently told of whoppers, one made thousands or even millions of times a day.

As an author, I promote my books by doing radio interviews on an almost-daily basis. These interviews don't just fall out of the sky. Being my own publicity department, I make all the arrangements, the phone being my main source of communication.

When calling the programming directors, I find that they may or may not be in their offices. If they are not, I get the commonly-worded phone message: "Hi, I'm either on the phone or away from my desk. Please leave your name and number, and I'll get right back to you."

Yeah, right.

Sometimes people will say that your call is "important" to them and ask you to please leave your name and number, etc. It then transpires that neither you nor your call were *that* important.

You were not the Pope or Nelson Mandela or Madonna.

Occasionally, you get the message where people say they'll "try" to get back to you. But they don't try. That's also a lie.

Sometimes, I will encounter a secretary or personal assistant, the human version of the answering machine: "Just leave your name and number with me, and we'll get right back to you," she will say.

Or she'll reply: "I'll relate your message to my boss, and he will get right back to you".

Those personal assistants know their bosses have never, ever, in their lives, returned a message—unless it was to some higher-up to whom they had to reply, or someone who could do something for them.

My only hope of getting in touch with elusive people is to keep calling back. Eventually, I might actually connect with the person who either likes my pitch or is likely to be, according to him or her "extreeeeeemely busy and unable to talk just then".

But then comes the inevitable: "Leave your name and number and I'll..." You know the rest.

Before becoming an author, I had my own advertising consultancy in which I was the writer, art director and account executive all rolled into one.

Cold calling was necessary if I wanted my family to eat. It isn't as difficult as you may think. You might struggle through the first two or three calls of the day, but after that, it's a breeze.

As a result of all my cold calling and all the landmines that come with the territory, I have developed compassion for solicitors of all kinds, always treating them as fellow human beings just trying to make a dollar and not the pests they are so commonly portrayed as.

I always thank them for taking the time to call,

even if I don't buy what they are selling. Friends who slam the phone down on solicitors think I'm nuts.

I've never had a phone slammed down on me, but of course you run the risk of getting some grouchy types on the phone biting your head off. I've encountered a few of those—like the woman at National Public Radio who barked at me that she was in a meeting.

Instead of being in my usual don't-take-it-personally mode, I blasted her back with: "Well, how the hell was I supposed to know you're in a meeting? Do you think I have X-Ray vision?"

That, as far as I can remember, was the only time I'd taken the bait. It's so easy to react to rudeness, but if my energy is high—and I make sure it is high through 20 minutes of meditation first thing in the morning—then I won't ever bark back.

These days, doing my author stuff, I recently figured out that I make between 90 to 125 calls a day, and yet only connect with five actual, living, breathing people.

The rest of my calls go to voicemail where I hear the offending message. But I rarely leave a name or number because, as I've said, these people NEVER return phone calls.

I think if they had a drop of integrity, they would leave a message something like this: "Hi, this is so and so, and if what you have to say interests me, and I think there is adequate reason for a future conversation with you that I will personally benefit from, I will call you back. And if you don't hear back from me, it's because I couldn't care less if you live or die."

With a message like that, a person might be shattered, disillusioned, disappointed, horribly depressed, stunned, given to sudden crying jags in crowded elevators and other public places, and even feel suicidal.

But at least a person would know where he or she stood.

7

"Hey, I was only kidding!"

You've had a stutter since your childhood and it shows up whenever you are under pressure. And you are extremely self-conscious about it.

So what do you say when the jokester in the office starts mimicking you?

This insensitive creep obviously doesn't care how deeply this might have hurt you, but he may be uneasily aware of disapproving bystanders. So his next words are likely to be the all too common: "Hey, I was only kidding."

It's "Hey, I was only kidding" when someone comments on your weight which has recently ballooned.

It's "Hey, I was only kidding," when your wife tells a group of friends that she only married you when her real true love married someone else.

And it's "Hey, I was only kidding," when someone says your feet are big enough to stamp out Chicago."

This kidding business is often said to be just teasing. "Hey, I was just teasing you. Lighten up!"

Or it's the putdown about not having a sense of humor: "What's wrong with you? Can't you take a joke?"

Or it's the sadist-turned-shrink: "Gee, you're so sensitive."

Or worse, the manipulative apology giver: "I

wouldn't have said that if I knew you were going to take offense. I love you. I wouldn't hurt you for the world. I was only kidding when I said your varicose veins made your legs look like roadmaps."

My thoughts about people who rake others over the coals is that they are, in truth, blood-thirsty bastards who pull wings off flies.

They use their mouths as one would use a saber, slashing and cutting whenever possible, especially when the prey is vulnerable.

"Hey, I was only kidding," is a good phrase to have on hand in case the person, as intended, shrivels up or starts crying.

How many times in your life have you been the butt of someone's nasty remarks?

What defense did you have? No doubt you were too flabbergasted at the time to come up with the proper retort, but may have come up with it hours or days after the incident. Meanwhile, you were fuming and in pain over what had been said to you.

When not able to think of an instant retort, a casual "go to hell" works wonders.

Or you can use any number of replies starting with the letter F.

But when attacked (and make no mistake—a verbal barb is an attack) such simple sayings don't come to mind.

One response that I like when being put down is a simple "ouch, that hurt".

Someone I worked with, the film director, Tony Scott, would issue a "oh, shaddap," with a big smile on his face. It was to the point, but not hostile.

I also like "Gee, I must have been wearing my DUMP HERE sign" which I attribute to my late wife, the wonderful Betty Bethards.

Nothing scares the bully/abuser more than being exposed as someone who has deliberately, viciously, hurt someone.

Yet people take it on the chin over and over again, not saying anything in return, until one day, all hell breaks loose. It's then they bust the tormentor one on the chops. Or worse.

In a recent study, it was shown that people who let loose with insults and jeers often hear the offending words in their heads before they utter them, and are then seemingly powerless to stop them from coming out of their mouths.

Severe mouth monitoring, or a long piece of duck tape needs to be deployed in this situation.

I was recently with a woman who did nothing but criticize me all evening. I finally told her, in as gentle a way as I could, that her stinging words, used on a more sensitive soul than myself, could really hurt that person.

"That's just too damned bad," she replied. "I speak the truth!"

"Well, maybe you could speak the truth on your own," I suggested, "in private, with no one else around..."

To be fair, all of us have made the occasional faux pas. A London friend of mine, Annie Farrow, was telling me how her mom, who lived in one of those lovely little villages in England, was having the new vicar in for tea.

"His nose entered the room before he did," Annie related. "It was the largest nose we had ever seen."

As her mother, on in years and mesmerized by this enormous appendage, was pouring the tea, she inquired: "And would you like cream with your nose?"

This kind of thing happens.

My ex-father-in-law, whose other son-in-law was someone named Simon Hernie, had a hard time not referring to him as Simon Hernia when introducing him to someone.

Annie Farrow's mother and my ex-father-in-law would never have added, "I was only kidding," to their statements, because there was no malicious intent involved. Approaching dementia, probably. And a lot of embarrassment.

It's the evil-doer who zooms in on another person's weak spot and then lets him or her have it that needs a lesson shown to him or her.

You might try: "Wow, the last time anyone saw a mouth like yours, it had a fish hook in it."

And then: "Hey, I was only kidding."

8

When road rage is justified.

Okay, it never is. But anyone who has ever driven a car has experienced it.

And it's a good thing that very few people act on it. Who needs a highway full of ranting, middle-finger waving motorists? Or worse, people with shotguns?

Not long ago, in the local newspaper, there was an item about some guy on the motorway who took a gun out of his glove compartment, leaned out the window, aimed, and shot the driver in the car behind him.

The bullet shattered the windshield of the other driver's car, and came to rest, lodged in the other driver's shoulder.

The reason for this assault? According to the apprehended shooter, the other driver had been relentlessly tail-gating him for the past 20 miles.

And even though I don't advocate shooting anyone, I do kind of understand the shooter.

Tail-gaters are some of the worst human beings on earth as far as I am concerned. They are dangerous and irresponsible and there should be a law that would take them off the road permanently.

Don't they have the common sense to know that if you have to stop short, they will have no chance to stop and will sail right into you? The answer is no.

But there is someone worse than the tail-gater, and

I'm not referring to a drunk driver, although he or she should also be taken off the road and never be allowed back.

Let me explain with a recap of what happened to me not so long ago.

I was zipping along on a two-lane country road in California, enjoying the scenery and the kind of feeling that comes with being on the open road temporarily free of responsibilities.

My destination was a resort in Pebble Beach, where I was planning to attend a convention.

At the speed I was traveling, I was sure that I would arrive at the hotel long before anyone else arrived, and that I would have plenty of time to rest and relax, even have a swim and sauna before dinner.

That's when I saw the stalled car ahead.

I have to admit that my next thought was selfish: Hell, it's not on a verge or anything. It's probably going to block the road for some time to come. Maybe even until a tow truck comes. And that could be hours!

Then, as I drew closer, I saw that the car wasn't broken down at all. It was actually moving, impercep-tibly, at way, way, way below the speed limit. As I got closer to the car, I had to decelerate and creep along.

Eventually, after a few minutes of this, I spotted something behind me that I hadn't noticed before. A line of about ten cars that had been zooming along like me, but now just creeping along the same way I was.

I had been repeatedly flashing my lights for him to pull into a lay-by to let us pass, and watched as he glid-ed by several. I thought that maybe he (or she) didn't see that I'd flashed my lights. It was a bright, sunny day, so the driver not seeing my flash was a possibility.

I flashed again, and again, nothing. There was ab-solutely no chance to pass him because the other lane with oncoming traffic was very busy, and there was a double yellow line. I was, by this time, getting rather agitated.

To pull around the car would have been worse than what this driver was doing. It would have been against the law and would have endangered many drivers and their passengers. So I flashed my lights once more, for a longer time. Either go faster or pull over, I was mentally instructing the driver. He (or she) appeared to be ignoring me.

Okay, I flashed my lights again, for an absurdly long time, being careful not to blind the drivers coming in the opposite direction. Again, no response. I figured that the driver could be so old as to not be cognizant of my flashing lights. I was going so slow, that I could have walked faster.

So now it was the horn, a very slight peep at first, but with that accomplishing absolutely nothing, a longer peep. The driver might not have seen my flashing light, but was he deaf, too?

Something I dislike as much as tailgating is using four letter words. But at this point, a few of them came jumping out of my mouth accompanied by another blast of the horn, this one at least 30 seconds. Yes, the driver must be deaf, I decided. I then found myself just leaning on the horn, just as the drivers behind me were leaning on theirs.

The cacophony we were making could have wakened the dead. Maybe we did jar a few folks out of their eternal rest as we passed a country cemetery, but it didn't even rouse the driver in the car ahead.

My next action, one that I deplore other drivers doing to me, as I explained earlier in this piece, was to tailgate. Maybe this would send out a message to the driver. It didn't.

I pulled back and for a very long time kept willing this road hog to either pull over in a lay-by or just turn off onto some side road or other. Those things didn't happen, either.

By now, I was imagining that the driver was some sort of power freak. He (or she) was, in my mind, an anti-social sadist enjoying the fact that he (or she) had an endless stream of cars with the drivers trailing behind. Isn't that some sort of power trip? I imagined a smile on the driver's face.

On most major highways in America, it is against the law to go too slowly, but on a dusty old back road, there are no cops hiding behind barns or haystacks ready to bounce. This was, unfortunately a dusty old back road.

After 20 minutes of this, I wanted to actually "bump" that car. That's what carjackers do. I wanted to bump him right off the road into a ravine. I would have felt justified. This driver was depriving me of my swim and sauna, and if he was to keep this crawl going, I might even miss dinner. And possibly the first night of the convention!

Going around a bend, I got a brief glimpse of the driver. He wasn't old at all. Probably around thirty, And he was smiling!

Now I really wanted to bash him. The worthless son of a bitch was holding up the world because he was a total loser, and this was his way of getting back at the world. My rational mind was also telling me that perhaps he was simply "unaware". I preferred my original assessment that he was a worthless son of a bitch.

To my left, I could see the fast-moving motorway, only there was no access onto it, except across a field of wheat. I considered just mowing across that, but decided against it.

In my rearview mirror, I observed that the driver directly behind me looked like he was just about to have cardiac arrest over this. What if I just stopped my car and ran up beside the road hog and yelled at him to pull over? Now, that was an insane idea, in keeping with my current mental state.

Finally, after what seemed an eternity, there was a branch in the road and this horrible person (I had decided that he was a wife-beater, child molester, arsonist, thief, and you name it) was turning off. I wanted to get a good look at him, but the angles of our cars didn't allow it. He just disappeared onto that other road.

Along with the rest of the cars behind me, I went from 10 miles to 50 miles per hour which felt like flying. This was heaven, this was bliss. I knew I would never make up for lost time, but at least we were moving.

And that's when I saw it ahead of me, a wreck. It was blocking the road. Only, as I found out, it was not a wreck...

9

People who offer to treat you to a meal.
After you've ordered.

Gee, if you knew you were going to be treated, you would have had what you really wanted.

Like most people, I've been to endless dinners and lunches and have picked up the tab many times. When treating, I always tell the other party that it is my treat and to have whatever they like, before they order. That way, they know it is an intended treat and not some kind of after-thought.

But when I am being treated, it is rare that this same courtesy is accorded. Of course, it is less expensive to let a person know after the meal that he or she is being treated, because some people will take advantage.

I've noticed that, on occasion, when I tell people I'm paying for the food, that their eyes automatically scrutinize the price column in search for the most expensive item on the menu.

One friend in particular, when being taken out to breakfast—where most dishes don't range much above $12.00—always manages to find a $20.00 item.

It's okay, though…I'm glad to provide this kind of fare. But I'm always amazed that a person can dare to order something so grand when the rest of us are having Cheerios.

Treating is one thing; going Dutch is another. Not long ago, a cousin from New York arrived in town for a series of business meetings and trade shows. He announced that he wanted to take a gourmet tour of the San Francisco Bay Area's most exclusive restaurants while he was here. That was fine, but as I found out, he wasn't intending to pay for any of his gourmet choices.

So because he was in my city, (and because I knew that if I didn't give him the royal treatment, he would return home and blab to all the relatives that I was cheap), I felt obliged to pay all the tabs, although I did manage to steer him away from the idea of eating at The French Laundry in Napa where the bill is never less than $500 for two.

The last time we met, it was at San Francisco's Moscone Convention Cnter where he had a booth at a trade show. This is where he made $126,000 in one afternoon. Afterwards, he asked me if I was free for dinner, and by this I figured he was inviting me out and was going to pay for a change.

As this was going to be our last meal this trip—he was flying home right after—I thought this to be a nice gesture on his part.

I didn't order from the right side of the menu, regardless of the fact that he owed me at least one great meal. I was extremely modest because even though I never personally made $126,000 in one afternoon, I didn't want him telling everyone in New York that I had landed him with a huge bill.

He went way overboard with the champagne and the pate and the Argentine quail stuffed with caviar. The bill came to a whopping $390.00, only $40.00 of which accounted for what I ate.

When it came time for paying for our dinner, he

didn't respond. It was as if he was in a sudden coma. I realized he was expecting me to pay again. Well, I now considered this a breach of etiquette—after all, he had asked me to dinner, and I was damned if I was going to pay. He could tell the family back in New York whatever he wanted. I just let the bill sit there. And sit there. And then he pulled a Cary Grant on me.

Okay, what is a Cary Grant? The story goes that when the actor Joel McCrea first came to Hollywood in the early 1930s, he and Cary Grant, now an established and steadily working screen idol, went out for lunch.

When the bill came, Joel, wanting to show Cary his appreciation for being taken under his wing, paid out of his paltry savings.

A few months later, the two had lunch again, and when the bill came and Cary ignored it, Joel again paid, even though he hadn't yet landed a part in a movie and was not in a position to fork out the dollars.

The next time they had lunch, Joel decided that it was now Cary's turn for sure. But Cary again ignored the bill. It just lay on the table between them for the longest time.

Finally, and much to Joel's relief, Cary reached over and picked up the bill, scanned it, and said in his inimitable Cary Grant voice:

"Let's go Dutch".

And this is what this cousin of mine said. I very graciously agreed, split the bill, and regretted that I had forgone an appetizer or dessert.

Needless to say, on my cousin's various trips back, I avoid having dinner, lunch, breakfast, coffee, or even tea with him.

10

Craze-making words: "Anything else I can help you with, Sir?"

The phone conversation with the salesperson at Schmoggins department store doesn't start right away. That's because I can't for the life of me get a salesperson at Schmoggins department store on the phone for 10 bloody minutes.

The phone prompts are the reason. First there's the electronic voice saying, "This is Schmoggins, your friendly department store, here to serve you. Your call is important to us, so please stay on the line and someone will be with you shortly."

This is followed by truly horrible music and the irritating and intermittent progress report stating that: "All our salespeople are helping customers (like I'm not a customer?), and the waiting time is 12 minutes. We apologize for the inconvenience, so please be patient, and someone will be with you as soon as possible."

Eventually, after much of my life has ebbed away, there's a voice on the other end, "Can I help you?"

I start to reply but am immediately aware that the voice on the other end isn't human: "Hi, my name is Cindy, and I'm the automated Schmoggins associate. Please tell me the reason for your call so that I can give you the satisfaction Schmoggins is known for. Let's get started. But first, please state the reason for your call."

Declining to answer because I know this will further delay me in getting to a live salesperson, Cindy, in her chirpy way, goes on to say, at least five times, that she is waiting for me to state the reason for my call.

Am I hurting Cindy's feelings by not replying? It sure feels that way around the fourth or fifth time. I might be imagining it, but Cindy, Shmoggins department store automated associate, sounds like she is taking my silence personally.

"I can't get you to the right department without knowing why you are calling," Cindy says, and there is no doubting it now, she is peeved.

After yet another protracted silence from me, Cindy says, clearly hurt, that she is putting me through to a live associate, that my call is being recorded for quality and assurance.

Finally there is someone on the line, a real person. Her name is Belinda, and she welcomes me to the Schmoggins Extremely Valued Customer and Quality Care department. For a moment, I say nothing because who knows, but this might be another trick where you think you are talking to a live person and find out it is the message machine again.

Finally finding my voice, I ask Belinda if she will put me through to housewares.

"Certainly, Sir. Right away, Sir, and thank you, Sir, for shopping at Schmoggins. And let me say, Sir, for all of us at Schmoggins, that we appreciate you as a customer and if there is anything we can do to make your telephone inquiries more effortless, please let us know."

It's probably easier to get through to the Pentagon than housewares because I spend at least 10 more minutes waiting. Interjected during my wait is the message that someone will be with me shortly.

This "shortly" business is getting on my nerves. There's nothing even remotely "shortly" about this. I've been trying to get through to housewares for 24 minutes. This is not "shortly". This is "extended long term".

Well, at least I haven't been cut off. Yet. That's something that happens all too often after you have spent what seems a lifetime getting this far.

But the phone is ringing! It's ringing! Please, I think, don't let it be a message machine. Something like: "You've reached the housewares department. No one is here to take your call. Please leave your name and number, and someone will get back to you as soon as possible. To reach the operator, please press zero."

The phone rings 14 times on the other end. I am now sure that there's no one there, and that I'm going to have to go through this whole frustrating exercise all over again. But then someone answers the phone. I can't believe it.

"Hello, this is Thomas in housewares. How can I give you the superb and satisfying customer service you so richly deserve?"

"Well, Thomas," I say, "you can give me the superb and satisfying customer service I so richly deserve by telling me why the vacuum cleaner I bought just the other day won't vacuum."

"So you bought a vacuum cleaner just the other day, and it won't vacuum? We haven't heard that complaint before."

Suddenly I'm in the wrong. Thomas hasn't heard that complaint before. It must be my fault that the vacuum isn't working—how else to explain it?

"So you got the vacuum home and assembled it? Did you then plug it in?"

"Like duh," I say in a goofy voice. "Is that the

funny looking thing with the prongs on the end? You plug it in???"

Thomas is not responding to my sarcasm. Even Cindy, the automated saleslady would have had more of a sense of humor.

"Obviously, your vacuum cleaner was assembled incorrectly," Thomas offers.

"I followed the directions exactly," I reply.

"Sir, we have customers calling every day telling us that something or other doesn't work, and we tell them to go back, take the item apart and then put it back together again."

"I followed the directions exactly," I repeat. "The damn thing doesn't work."

"Do you have the vacuum cleaner with you right now?"

"No, I'm on my cell phone in the car and I don't carry my vacuum cleaner with me when I'm driving."

"Well, I will need the name of the item," Thomas says.

"It's a DirtClinger 550."

"And the serial number?"

"I don't know the serial number."

"Well, I can't access the information without the serial number," Thomas says. "I suggest that you call back when you have the serial number."

"Why do you need the serial number? Aren't all these vacuum cleaners alike?

"As I say, there is no way I can access the information without the serial number."

"Look, can't you do some trouble-shooting to see what might be the problem?"

"Not without the serial number."

By now, I want to kill Thomas. I know that a serial number isn't going to prove anything one way or the other. But I can't do anything about this. I have just wasted 40 minutes out of my day.

"You know, I have a good mind to just return this piece of junk and get a refund," I say, making this sound like a threat.

"That is definitely an option and entirely up to you," Thomas replies briskly. "As long as you have the receipt and you've disassembled the item and have it placed in the box exactly as you received it, I see no reason why you can't return it. And we have an excellent selection of vacuums for you to choose from if you wish to replace it."

Frustrated, I consider asking to speak to the supervisor, but something tells me I won't have any satisfaction. And just as I'm about to hang up, Thomas asks if I would like to answer a few questions regarding customer satisfaction. Considering that I haven't had any satisfaction, this statement is right out of the theatre of the absurd. I'd much rather wrap the receiver around this salesclerk's head.

"You've gotta be kidding," I say.

Thomas is trained to detach from customer hostility. He doesn't appear to have heard me. "Well, thank you for choosing Schmoggins for your shopping needs," he continues. "I hope you found our service to your liking and that all your questions were answered.

And then, he says them, the words that might have got him killed had this been an in-person exchange: "Anything else I can help you with?"

11

When friends suggest you all go out for drinks, dinner, and dancing.

At *your* house.

That lovely old custom known as "the dinner party" seems to have drifted into culinary history, undoubtedly spurred into extinction by the lack of reciprocation.

My wife, Betty, and I always used to host a New Year's party which was quite lavish. We'd invite mostly the same friends year after year...but never found ourselves invited to as much as a grilled cheese sandwich at their homes.

So one year we just quit giving this annual New Year's bash. People were shocked, confused and disoriented. And then came outright anger. We had inconvenienced the whole lot of them.

They were even more shocked when they heard we were going on a cruise, instead. We would be at sea happily ignoring Christmas, Hanukkah, Kwanzaa, and that most important occasion of all: The Solstice at New Year's.

Everything leading up to this decision was fraught with guilt. We were, after all, abandoning our circle. Fear rose up in us that they wouldn't speak to us again, and there was the uncertainty as to whether or not that this was the right thing to do.

All that was small change compared to our feeling of liberation when we'd ducked out of the same old one-sided rut. Pure exhilaration resulted. What, in the first place, made us think that New Year's Eve wouldn't be celebrated if we didn't give a party? Did we think the new year would pass unnoticed and that Times Square would cancel the descending ball?

As for the people we'd invited year after year, it seemed that ending our spate of New Year's parties and all the other yearly get-togethers was, concurrently, the end of our associations with those folks because most of them never got in touch.

All those kisses on the cheeks, all those warm hugs, all those expressions of love and affection, so generously displayed by these former guests when they would enter our home? Gone forever.

We were then left with a skeletal crew of friends and acquaintances...until it became apparent that even they weren't all that keen on getting together, especially when we suggested meeting at a local restaurant. We were the folks that had always provided gourmet meals for them, and now we were suggesting...a restaurant???

There was something else going on with our friends. Much as we didn't want to face it, we realized that they were playing the field, stalling us, holding out for a better offer.

They would ply us with excuses for not getting back to us right away. It would be that they had sudden visitors who would be with them for a month, or how they were on some diet or other that didn't actually allow them to *eat food*, or how they weren't sure if George would be on a business trip to Outer Albania or not, or if his wife, Trish, was going to be busy putting in a concrete patio all by herself.

In the sincerest of voices, these alleged friends would ask. "Can we let you know in a week or so?" And then they would never get back to us.

But not all is lost. Today, we have great fun with the friends who are left.

Both of them.

12

Tax auditors and how they terrorize people.

Not long ago, I was notified by letter that I was to report to my regional IRS office in Santa Rosa, California for an audit.

I was told in a letter, which is not the same thing as being asked, to be there at a certain time on a certain date, the implication being that my failing to show up would result in a fine or imprisonment or both.

Complying with the order, I arrived promptly at the appointed time, carrying a briefcase of relevant documents including my tax return records from each of the previous five years.

The receptionist at the front desk was very pleasant, leaving me to wonder how anyone who worked for the IRS could have such a sunny personality. Especially since people were getting slaughtered in the adjacent offices.

As I was ushered into one of those offices, a wreck of a man was being ushered out. He needed a stretcher. What had they done to him in there? I glanced down at his hands to see if he still had his fingernails.

This was the first IRS audit that I was handling personally. In previous years, my accountants always took care of such matters, so I didn't know why I was handling the audit instead of them. They knew what they were doing. I didn't.

"Mr. Rubin?" the slightly-built man asked. He was wearing a gray suit and rimless glasses and a facial expression that said, "I have ways of making you talk".

He could have saved that facial expression for somebody else. I didn't have anything to hide. All my business dealings were 100% above-board, and my deductions totally legit, so why did I feel like a combination of Al Capone and Bernie Madoff?

"May I see last year's tax return?" he asked. I handed it over. He studied it. And studied it. I had no place to look. This was a windowless office. There were no cheerful posters on the wall to focus on. My eyes were going crazy.

Once or twice I gave a tiny cough just to make sure I was alive. There was no air in the room.

Finally, he looked up and said: "I see you didn't make much of a profit last year in your business. What is it, publishing? You spent more money printing books than you made in selling them.

What kind of books are these?"

"Spiritual," I said. "One of them is a book on dream analysis, another on developing your intuition and another…"

"I see," he cut in. So this publishing company, it's your hobby?"

Hobby? I worked very hard to get where I was as a publisher and this little squirt was calling it a hobby? Well, I just wish I had said what I should have said, "Is your job your hobby?" But I only thought up that comeback many hours later.

He continued to grill me. Every single item on my deductions list was questioned. The nit-picking was tedious and time consuming, but eventually, he seemed satisfied. Or so he said.

"I have to now confer with my supervisor on your

'situation' and will be back shortly." He got up taking all my papers with him and leaving me to stare at the wall and wonder at my fate. He was back in twenty minutes.

"We have decided to disallow all your deductions," he announced.

Now, I'm a writer, and I should know words, but for some very strange reason, I thought the word "disallow" was a fancy way of saying "allow".

I thanked the auditor like he was the nicest guy on earth.

"This is wonderful," I said. "I am so relieved. Thank you very, very much…"

The guy just looked at me like I was truly mental. I extended my hand which he gazed at as one would gaze at a dead fish, but finally took it. I practically shook his arm out of its socket.

Walking to the car, I thought that it had all turned out very well! But as I was driving, the word "disallow" stuck in my brain and by the time I got home, I realized this word meant "not allow".

Not allow? They were not going to allow any of my deductions??? I couldn't believe it.

That meant the office telephone and electricity, the vast printing costs I'd accrued, research expenses, office supplies, the new computer, car expenses, internet service, postal expenses, cell phone expenses, books, magazines, newspapers, Federal Express, tolls and parking, new locks on the office door, advertising, domain expenses, business travel, business car rentals, plane fares, hotels, restaurants, client entertaining, business travel, new printer, insurance, trade shows…none of these would be deducted?

Without these deductions, I would be in financial hot water. I did what I usually did when faced with a serious situation, I panicked.

My one hope was to call my accountants…which I did.

"We'll deal with this," they said.

As their office was in San Rafael, California and not Santa Rosa, they got the case transferred to their area, and after their meeting with the auditors (at which I was not present), they got all my deductions through.

One day, about a month later, I was stopped at a red light in Santa Rosa, when the auditor with whom I'd originally dealt with walked in front of my car. He did a double take as he noticed me. I was the nut who thanked him so profusely for his decision to "disallow" my deductions.

Had he had his way in regard to disallowing my deductions I might have, as he passed my car, gunned the motor, the next best thing to actually running him down. But instead, I just put on a truly insane facial expression with my eyes crossed and my tongue hanging out, and waved.

13

The improper usage of the "F" word.

I'm having lunch in a London restaurant called Lacys with Alistair, an art director friend who is abusing his expense account.

The owner of Lacys is the highly respected food journalist, Marguerite Costa, whose columns have appeared regularly in such magazines as Bon Appetite and Gourmet.

A formidable woman approaching sixty or so, Marguerite has recently opened her Pimlico restaurant with a view to providing the very best in French cuisine and wine.

If Alice Waters is known for pioneering the art of healthy, organic cuisine, Marguerite strives for exactly the opposite. Health food, to her, is not something fit for human consumption. Her menu is literally food to die for...so rich, so artery-clogging...so French, with the heavy creams and other ingredients that many of today's food pundits claim will destroy you.

But if you are going to die, the accompanying wine list is huge and tempting. So tempting, in fact, that Alistair (born cockney in Hackney, but aspiring for an 'establishment' image) has decided that we should have a different bottle for each course.

"We'll start with the Salon Mesnil champagne" Alistair tells the waiter. "And would you ask Madame

Costa if she would share a glass with us?"

Beckoned to entertain her clientele, Marguerite, in a chiffon-like flowing dress and with her hair piled in a bun atop her head, appears a few moments later, saying, in a plummy voice, that it will, indeed, be her pleasure.

As people will, when in the throes of the higher realms of a quality setting, we discuss the various erudite subjects people talk about. Then I ask: "Have you ever met Fanny Cradock?"

Fanny Cradock was, at one time, a British TV phenomenon, a somewhat crass-seeming chef who'd captivated her audience much in the same way as the much gentler sing-songy Julia Child once did hers in the U.S.A.

"Oh yes," Marguerite says, in her plummy, high octave voice and with perfect BBC diction "We were at a convention together, and some people gathered me up and delivered me to her Royal Highness, Fanny Craddddddock."

"You'd never met her before that?" I ask.

"Oh yes, we had gone to culinary college together. But Fanny wasn't about to acknowledge that fact. Instead, she just looked me up and down and finally said, 'Oh yes, I thinnnnkkkk I've heard of you'. At which point I thought to myself 'well, FUCK YOU' and walked off."

To me, Marguerite's use of the F-word, in contrast with her lady-like demeanor and her finishing school accent, was the proper way to treat probably the most controversial word in the world, a word that should only be rolled out when the occasion warrants it.

So many people let it pop out of their mouths so often that it permeates the air with reckless abandon. This being the case, it is in danger of losing its full force.

And what is it with comics who pound it into the ground? Do they think this is really funny? Please, bring back Bob Hope, Carol Burnett, Jack Benny, Lucille Ball, Johnny Carson, Milton Berle.

The word should be used sparingly, and in the way Marguerite used it regarding Fanny Cradock.

On the other hand, whereas Marguerite used it as a put down, and rightly so (Fanny did come over as a bitch of the first water and, in fact, was eventually fired from her TV show); it should really be used as a special greeting.

"Fuck you," one person might cheerfully say to another. "And you," would be the chipper response, because what greater wish is there than that a person should have a fulfilling and fabulous sexual experience?

In Japan, when people are bowing toward one another, they could be saying "Fuck you, fuck you…"

An expression of gratitude in any language might go something like: "Thank you and may you be eternally fucked."

The history of the word is quite fascinating. Experts claim that it's of British origin, although there is proof of a German strain or influence.

Whatever it's origin, it has become an overused, international, multitasked word. You can be fucked up (confused, disorganized, the victim of some unfortunate happening) and you can be fucked out (exhausted).

Something can be a SNAFU (A WWII term originated by American soldiers meaning, Situation Normal All Fucked Up).

Some people will use it in an inquiry as in "What the fuck are you doing here?"

Another person might say "Get the fuck out of

here," as if a fuck is an entity or animal.

These terms are a part of today's lexicon for people of all ages. And then, regretfully, it is used in the worst possible taste when attached to somebody's mother.

At any rate, it's a word that's here to stay. And so in closing, I think it appropriate to say, in the very best possible sense and with your continual well-being at heart:

"Fuck you."

14

Teachers and professors who shouldn't be allowed in a classroom.

When I was taking a writing class at Columbia University, I told the professor that I was going to write a short story that would remind the reader of an Henri Rousseau painting.

Instead of saying that this was an interesting idea, she got exasperated, a typical reaction of hers and typical of the way she had regarded me from day one.

While all the other students in her class were aspiring New Yorker Magazine types who wrote stories that were beautifully executed, I wrote raw stories of people on the street, junkies looking for a fix, that kind of thing.

And, also, stories that were supposed to remind the reader of a Henri Rousseau painting.

From what I knew of this professor, she had spent all her career in New York working in the literary agencies and on various magazines. Aside from one period of time during WWII when she lived in Los Angeles and had had a rumored affair with Greta Garbo, she had edited an anthology of the best short stories since Edgar Allan Poe. It was for this latter achievement that she was best known.

As the "grande-dame" of Columbia's English department, she had a penchant for telling people what was right and what was wrong about their style (she could bang away at bad grammar and sentence structure and all of that—this didn't bother me). Nor was I bothered that she continually used me as an example of how "not to write".

I'd had teachers like her all my life, and I knew how to keep my balance through controlling the situation. My method for doing this was via the agency of humiliation, or, in more simplistic terms, seeing a professor squirm.

I was heartless in that regard. As an avid reader of just about everything, old and new, I would ask this professor, in class, if she'd read the latest, greatest, novelist whomever he or she might be, or even a classic by Rimbaud.

Invariably, she hadn't. And I would say imperiously: "You havennnnnn't???"

In terms of writing herself, it was my haughty opinion that since she hadn't produced even one word in published print, what right had she to teach a class? And to criticize other people's endeavors the way she did?

The other thing about this class was that, because I didn't seem to give a damn about anything and was a comedian, the other students liked me a lot. I was aware that they even looked up to me, wanting my thoughts of their work over the professor's. They regarded me as a shaker-upper.

Just as I approved of the fine work they were doing, they approved of my desire to break the mold and go where no writer had ever gone before.

Of course, I learned over time that nothing was ever going to be new again, that everything new was just something faded from memory that became recycled.

But at the time of my stint at Columbia University, I thought I would capture a whole new genre in the decades after. It didn't happen that way for me. I was innovative in a way I never expected.

Needing to make some money, I took what was to be a temporary job as a copywriter in an ad agency. It just happened to be an agency that helped—along with a handful of others in New York—to totally re-invent the ad business in a way that utilized the incredible creativity of, in the beginning, just a small group: Bob Gage, Phyllis Robinson, Helmut Newton, Bill Bernbach, George Lois, Jerry DellaFemina, Mary Wells, and Carl Ally.

No one had ever seen advertising like this before. It was open, honest, ironic, funny, meaningful, and powerful.

In this unique environment—nothing like the dismal working atmosphere of the popular TV series "Madmen"—the job of copywriters such as myself, and art directors on the same wave length, was to grab consumers in a way that said, "We are not trying to pull the wool over your eyes. We will express life's ironies. We will make you laugh. We will be eye-openers on the world's greatest problems with solutions on how to remedy them. We will never advertise something that is bad for you."

As it turned out during this all-too-short period in ad history when consumers preferred to watch TV commercials, rather than the programs they were sponsoring, I had chosen my life's work.

I can honestly say that in that genre, I followed the masters and did work that was often on a par with theirs. It was extremely satisfying even after the creative revolution had passed, and those of us who'd been so much a part of it were still carrying on the traditions.

But back when I was in the writing class at Columbia University and when I'd made my comment about wanting to write a story that would be like a Rousseau painting, I had no idea why those words came out of my mouth.

As a teenager going to Charles Evans Hughes High School (formerly Textile Straubenmuller High School) on West 18th Street in Manhattan, I would cut classes and practically live in the Museum of Modern Art. One of the paintings that held me spellbound was 'The Sleeping Arab" by Henri Rousseau.

In this painting, an Arab is definitely sleeping while standing over him is a ferocious lion. Viewing this painting, one has to consider that which is about to happen. Will the lion devour the sleeper? It kinda looks that way.

The Museum of Modern Art, in those days, was just the right size, not too small, not too large. Not at all the way it is today where you can't possibly take in, on a single visit, all the art that's available.

Cutting class to visit Rousseau was an important venture for me. It was also a way to escape the teachers at my school who thought of me as retarded (it was true that I was dyslexic and couldn't learn anything). They never failed to remind me how dumb I was.

Maybe that's where I got in the habit of later challenging my college professors. This habit probably began when I was as a 13 year old high school freshman. Our English class assignment was to write a two-page report on some book or other, but I wrote something far more ambitious.

I can't imagine now what compelled me, but in the week or 10 days that it was due, I wrote an actual novel titled, "The Red Tape Murder Mystery".

It was then that my English teacher, Mrs. Greenfield, a woman of about fifty, leaned back in her chair and announced to me, in front of the entire class, that I was a moron.

My response was to calmly inform her that I wanted to return the compliment. When I think about it now, I am amazed at my cool headedness in handling this situation. Especially since I could have landed in the principal's office for talking back in such a manner.

Had this incident occurred in this day and age, Mrs. Greenfield's comment might have landed her in a lot of trouble because times have changed and teachers cannot verbally abuse their students without experiencing the wrath of the parents, school officials, protest groups, and the media.

But Mrs. Greenfield took no action. She did not send me down to the principal's office. Sometime later, perhaps after a month or two, she, again focusing on me, announced in front of the entire class that she had changed her mind and that I was not, after all, a moron.

I didn't know what had made her call me a moron in the first place and, in retrospect, shocking as it was, I hadn't taken it all that seriously. On this occasion, seeing that Mrs. Greenfield was holding out the olive branch, I replied that I never thought that she was a moron, either.

I will never know for sure what made Mrs. Greenfield change her mind about me. I can only assume that in seeing more of my writing, she decided she'd made a brash assumption, and that, indeed, my work was original and that I was a weird genius of sorts.

Unfortunately, my other teachers didn't share Mrs. Greenfield's new found respect for me. In fact, I was considered the school idiot for the rest of my time there and with good reason.

I simply could not learn the conventional way.

There was a certain Mr. Urdang whom I remember especially well for his brand of cruelty, his specialty being the fast, sharp, lethal verbal one-two punch.

It was my senior year, and I don't know how I even got to be a senior, I volunteered to work on the class yearbook. Joining the committee for our first meeting, I saw that the other students were strictly of the "honor" type, none with whom I was friendly.

Mr. Urdang, a math teacher who'd had his toes shot off in WWI, and who was in charge of getting the yearbook organized, surveyed the group and seeing me, the school idiot, told me to "get up and get out". It was an extremely horrible moment, with the honor students smirking and all eyes on me as I left the room.

In a state of anguish, I immediately went to the auditorium and started playing the piano. This instrument, which I had played by ear since the age of three (couldn't learn to read music), had always been my destination in times of turmoil and this was definitely one of those times.

I have no idea where the music that came out of my fingers came from. It was as if Dave Brubeck had taken over my body. I was in a completely "other worldly" state and as I played, people started coming into the auditorium, teachers and students alike, all silent and in awe as I, lost in the music, played on and on.

When finally I finished, to deafening applause, I got up and walked up the aisle, still in some sort of trance and almost unaware of the people cheering me, but I did see Mr. Urdang amongst the crowd—whom I totally ignored.

A postscript to that episode is that practically all of the cartoons in the yearbook were mine, and I enjoyed seeing them until the day I angrily burned the book on a bonfire.

I probably would still be in high school to this day were it not for the fact that Mrs. Greenfield eventually became the Dean of Students. When it was time for me to graduate, I was surprised to see my name with those who had passed their final exams and would be graduating.

Now there is no way in hell that I could have passed my final exams. In the biology exam, for instance, I wrote of two amoebas meeting, introducing themselves, and after a decent interval, having a child.

Also, there were a number of teachers up in arms because I, a white guy, was dating a Puerto Rican girl whom I would be escorting to the prom.

My geography teacher, Mrs. Snitow, actually asked me if it was true that I was taking Zoraida Rivera to the prom.

My answer had been a distinct "Si!"

It was Mrs. Greenfield, I have always assumed, who said "let us graduate this person. If we don't, he'll be in high school till he's 80 years old. He is never going to pass an exam."

Thank you, Fritzi Greenfield, wherever you are. I know you left this planet some years ago (I went back to the school 15 years after graduation and was told).

Mrs. Greenfield, you believed in me. But the other teachers didn't. And maybe that's why my writing professor at Columbia was getting it in the neck.

"You do know who Henri Rousseau was, don't you?" I'd asked. She didn't.

I'd written the story which had nothing whatsoever to do with a sleeping Arab and read it aloud in class. It was about a starving young girl, someone hooked on heroin who, penniless, goes into a New York deli and just looks at the food in the display case.

The woman behind the counter is very brusque and eventually tells the girl that it's closing time. But the woman then realizes that this food would have to be replaced for the next day and offers it to the girl. For some inexplicable reason, the girl takes offense when the woman tells her it will only go into the garbage, and stabs her to death.

Okay, this was not a very good story, and there was every reason to fail me on it, but that's not the point. The point is that, unbelievably, one of the other students, a dark haired girl, usually quite reserved, spoke up. "I don't know why," she said, "but this story reminds me of an Henri Rousseau painting."

By this time in our relationship, my writing teacher was so fed up with me, she screamed at the girl. "Admit it. He told you to say that. He enlisted you in his plan to humiliate me, to make me look stupid!"

"No, he didn't," the girl assured her. "It's just as I say, this story reminds me of an Henri Rousseau painting."

Several weeks later, Our grades were posted on the door of the classroom. Sure enough, I got an F. Rather than seeing this as something disastrous, something that I could have appealed, I saw it as a victory.

To this day, I am proud of that F.

15

The inability to see what they might be doing to your food in a restaurant kitchen after you've complained about it and sent it back.

If you only knew what goes on in many restaurant kitchens, you would never step foot in a restaurant again.

But if you really want to risk your stomach, intestines and colon, just go ahead and complain about a meal.

Sending it back to the kitchen won't be fatal, although you may wonder why the steak that was too rare now has a heel print in it.

Restaurant workers, including chefs, are notorious for taking out their frustrations on your food.

In many instances, these workers see their customers as a mass of hungry cattle for whom they reserve their greatest contempt. If one of the herd tells a waiter that the fish fillet he has ordered is still frozen, not only will the fish fillet come back fully thawed, but there might be an extra ingredient like the chef's saliva. Spitting on and in food is said to be common.

Urinating in food isn't unknown. I saw it with my own eyes, not in a restaurant, but in a Marine Corps mess hall kitchen.

The cook thought it was funny to urinate in a huge

vat of scrambled eggs. His pissing in the eggs pissed off some onlookers who reported the incident and the cook was duly court-martialed, not because his actions toward the unsuspecting Marines was so disgusting, but because he was destroying government property—all those eggs.

During summer breaks when I was in college, I worked as a waiter in various resorts. A customer, not my own, complained one evening that his steak was tough. His waiter returned it to the chef who took it, flung it on the floor, jumped on it, put it back on the plate, added a sprig of parsley, and had it delivered back to the customer with his apologies. The customer said it was now "just right" and enjoyed it immensely.

Every once in a while, food authorities will pounce on a restaurant and fine the owners for any misdemeanors.

Not long ago, there was a case in New York City where 13 Chinese restaurants were discovered skinning and deboning rats. The rat's bodies were, in one case, on the cutting board, ready for dissection, when the authorities arrived.

After reading an account of this in the newspaper, I vowed never again to order anything that looked like beef in a Chinese restaurant. But then I forgot and ordered beef and broccoli in a restaurant on Bleeker Street.

Just as it arrived, I remembered the article. I looked down at the beef, and it looked like it was breathing. Naturally, I couldn't take even one bite.

"Anything wrong?" the waiter asked in a singsongy voice...

"No," I said, "if I can just have the bill..."

"Not hungry?'

"No, just the bill."

"You want something else? Egg foo yong?"

"Just the bill."

And you know those notices in restrooms that ask kitchen personnel to wash their hands after relieving themselves? Forget it.

I've seen executive chefs come out off stalls and leave the restroom without washing their hands.

I've even reported a few.

So what's the alternative to eating in a restaurant? Eating at home? Sometimes that can be even more dangerous.

Foods spoil, and we're not aware of it, even if the expiration date is in bold type.

There's just as much bacteria on your kitchen counter as there is on a restaurant kitchen counter. And salmonella is extremely democratic.

One other problem is hair. In days of old, anyone working in a hotel or restaurant kitchen was required to wear a hair net. Whatever happened to that ruling? Everyone loses hair. It just falls out. Hotel and restaurant kitchens are not off limits.

Try this test at home. Get some black carpeting and walk on it a couple of times a day. At the end of the week, you will see a ton of hair.

There'll also be dried bits of scalp.

How would you like an unasked for side order of dried scalp on your tuna melt?

Yeah, yeah, I know…it's protein.

But aside from eating, what other dangers lurk when you are at the mercy of others in a public place?

How about hotels and motels? According to a study, there are more germs in a hotel room than there are in a hospital. Were you to see what might be occupying that room, besides yourself, you would be grossed out.

You think the sheets are always changed, for instance? Forget it. What about those coverlets? How often do they clean those besides maybe never?

The documentary I saw advised viewers to refrain from touching anything in a hotel room and bathroom, including the light switch, the faucet knobs, the toilet handle, the toilet paper. That's right. You know the fold motel and hotel maids make on the toilet roll so as not to have to replace it with a fresh roll? It's crawling.

By the way, you might want to investigate what unwelcome guests are living in your home. They are usually the same ones found in a hotel.

There is one really effective resistance fighter within our bodies to cope with all the germs we encounter on a given day. That's an immune system that's in working order. It's our own internal health department.

It allows us to stay in hotels without fatal consequences and to eat in restaurants.

But even with such protection, please, don't send back that hamburger because it happens to be too rare.

16

People who ask your honest, honest opinion. And then never talk to you again after you've given it.

Somebody asks you what you think about this or that and suddenly you're an expert. But before you start dispensing your wisdom, it's a good idea to consider: What does this person really want of you?

Are you being asked to massage someone's ego? Give a flowery and flattering summation? Or is the request based on giving well thought out, constructive criticism that will sincerely aid the person?

About a year ago, an extremely accomplished jazz harpist/pianist and friend, Sparky Cole, sent me her latest CD, and asked me to critique it.

She is one of the most talented musicians I have ever had the pleasure of hearing, and I was honored that she wanted my opinion on this particular CD.

Her request was worded in such a way that expressed how appreciative she would be if I would do this for her. She asked that I listen objectively, to hold nothing back, and to feel free to share exactly what I thought, bad or good, of the CD.

So I did.

I told her, first of all, I loved her exquisite musicianship, but that maybe there was perhaps something unbalanced in the studio mix because the female singer she collaborated with was so loud and brassy that her delicate, harp accompaniment was fairly drowned out.

Not only that, but that the singer was performing in a completely different genre—in the blues style—while Sparky's music was light and almost classical in its presentation.

And so I confidentially emailed my remarks, and then waited for Sparky's response.

And waited.

And waited.

What became obvious after about a month was that my statement to Sparky had not met with her approval. I had mistaken what it was she really wanted which had nothing whatsoever to do with my listening objectively to the CD, holding nothing back, or feeling free to share that which I thought, bad or good, of her CD.

Puzzled, and also sensing that I had lost Sparky as a friend, I phoned her and left a message. When I got no reply, I phoned again and got no reply. I then emailed twice and sent a Christmas card.

I never heard from Sparky again. I had to face it. She had dumped me.

This was the result of giving Sparky the honest opinion she'd requested.

Prior to this experience, it had been my practice to never to open my mouth without being asked.

It is surprising how many people give you their opinions without being asked, especially in New York, where people have no qualms about telling you how tired you look or how you should never wear that color, and so on.

It happens in other places as well. I remember walking on an overgrown tropical trail in Hawai'i with a group of hikers. I was the only one wearing jeans while everyone else wore shorts or bathing suits. Because of this, I was roasting in the heat and humidity.

Deciding that I'd had enough, I turned around and headed back when a woman, coming in my direction commented "that's what you get for wearing jeans."

"You're always so critical," I replied to this woman whom I had never seen before, and walked on, not even glancing back but seeing her in my mind's eye her just standing there, stumped, wondering where she had met me before and how I could have known her so well.

It is my belief that people who never offer an opinion are the ones who succeed in life. If people can't figure out what you think about anything, you create a mysterious and powerful aura around yourself.

So now, even if I am asked, even if I am begged, even if I am promised some great reward for my opinion, I will waffle. I will change the subject. I will make believe I have had a sudden loss of hearing.

But Sparky, if you are reading this, and I hope you are, (because I've sent you a copy of this book), I want you to know that I really like you and your work.

But really, that last CD was terrible.

17

Those who get up early on a Sunday morning.

And think you should, too.

One of the ways to deal with everyday crisis and happenings is to hang on for Sunday morning when you can sleep late.

Or, at least, try to.

Recently, I've been plagued by people who think nothing of interrupting this sacred time of rejuvenation, renewal, and well-being by waking you out of your blissful slumber.

Today, it's Sheldon Weingarten on the phone, a golf partner. He's a big, goofy guy, like the guys who play the sidekick on those dumb TV sitcoms but never the leading man.

For Chrissakes, Sheldon, it's six in the morning..."

"So, are you going to sleep all day?" he replies.

Up until that moment, I'd been in a deep, deep, coma-like sleep, during which time my battered brain and body were in recovery mode from the unbelievably horrendous week I'd just barely survived.

After telling Sheldon how he can reproduce all by himself, I fall back asleep. Until the phone rings again

12 minutes later.

This time it's someone from Larchmont, New York calling me here in California for donations to a charity in Larchmont where my niece, Linda, lives.

On recent a visit to Larchmont to see Linda, I had made a generous contribution at her charity's fundraising event and now there's this guy on the phone wanting even more.

I don't believe in capital punishment except for people who call me early on a Sunday morning. Life in prison without parole being is next choice.

To my way of thinking, a person cannot be any more obnoxious, antisocial, and maladjusted than to call someone on a Sunday morning before noon. Ignorance of time zones is no excuse.

Instead of hanging up on this guy, I contain my anger and ask him if he knows what time it is on my end. He doesn't. I inform him.

"Oh," he says. "Well, I'm calling from New York where it's 9:15 and I thought it was 9:15 where you are."

"And you know where I am?

"No, not exactly. I don't usually check time zones; takes too long." And then he just continues on with his spiel without any kind of apology, and as if he hasn't committed a serious crime.

"I am hanging up now," I say, wondering if the way I crash my phone down might cause him a permanent hearing disorder for life. I am sincerely hoping so.

Getting back to sleep for the third time never has the same quality about it after you've been awakened so brutally twice before. Never do you return to that lush limbs-floating sensation. But I do manage to reconnect, after a struggle, with the nether-world. Then the phone rings again!

Some guy wants to know if his girlfriend Daphne is there.

"Yes," I say, "and I'm screwing her right now."

Many people turn off their phones before going to sleep. I could do that, but what if I've won a million dollars in a contest and the contest people are trying to get in touch with me?

What if all they can only get is my message machine and what if they don't want to leave word? What if they just go on to the next number on their list and give MY million dollars to someone else?

Stuff like that happens. And I don't want to be the person stuff like that happens to.

It is an option for me, however, to ax Sheldon Weingarten, my overbearing, in-your-face, golf-playing partner. And any other so-called friends who don't give a damn what time they call.

After all the calls on this particular Sunday morning, I've devised a plan.

In an overly sweet, pleasant, solicitous, and patient tone that bespeaks a gracious manner, the idea is to get their phone numbers and sincerely promise to call them back.

And then to make sure the promise is kept.

On a Sunday morning.

Before dawn!

18

Young folks who assume gray hair and wrinkles mean senility.

When I was younger, I kinda made those assumptions, too. Now, I'm ashamed of it. For instance, there was the time when Mrs. Cottle, my girlfriend's mother, came to visit her daughter, Lee-Ann, in California. She was very excited about their planned trip to Yosemite National Park.

"Oh," I said, "you just missed Yosemite. It's went on tour...36 cities in 36 days..."

"It did?" Mrs. Cottle asked, obviously very disappointed.

"Yes," I said, hardly able to get the words out before falling into a screaming fit of laughter.

When the laughter finally wore off, and both Lee-Ann and her mother were glaring at me, I had a sudden, rare, pang of conscience. This sweet woman really believed me and didn't even question the logistics of transporting the hundreds of acres and the majestic mountain peaks, not to mention the 40 story-high waterfalls of Yosemite National Park from city to city.

Today, being older, I find that more than a few gray hairs of my own seems to attract scam artists who ply their artful dodger rhetoric in my direction.

Not long ago, I was having some repairs made on the outside of my house. The young man doing the work told me that all the wood trimmings would have to be replaced because that was something homeowners were supposed to do every couple of years.

Obviously, this young man was mistaking me for Mrs. Cottle because there was absolutely nothing wrong with the wood trimmings on my house.

But when you think of it, how many older people are swindled each year by people who deem them as doddering or decrepit?

At one time, again when I was very young (and after being dumped by Lee-Ann), I lived in Honolulu, and the only job I could get was that of selling "Paradise of the Pacific Magazine" door to door.

It was a very good deal for me because, during the training period of three weeks, I was housed and fed in a beautiful mansion in Makiki Heights.

Each day, after a full and satisfying breakfast, I would follow an experienced trainer from door to door, watch his technique, and take notes.

My trainer was a guy called Artie whose presentation was fast and convincing. He would ring a doorbell and then engage the person in polite talk before offering the magazine absolutely free.

Then, after Artie had made a case for the magazine being something a person couldn't live without, he would ask an exorbitant fee for handling and mailing. This handling and mailing fee was, as I realized, an outrageous increase in price. Were the person to simply buy the publication off a magazine rack, the savings would have been half.

Feeling uncomfortable that this might be a scam, I nevertheless went along with it anyway because I loved being housed and fed in Makiki Heights.

So each day, I would trudge along Artie as he went from house to house. One of the people opening his door to Artie was an old guy with only one leg. He'd been at Pearl Harbor during the attack and had lost his leg and one eye at Guadalcanal. He seemed lonely, and pleased that someone, like Artie, would take an interest in him.

"Sir, you are a hero, a true American hero, and I'm honored to meet you and shake your hand," Artie had said, but all this "interest" seemed just a way to soften the guy up so that he would take the magazine subscription.

I knew this was wrong and tried to dissuade Artie from continuing this charade. This interference met with an angry shove that landed me three or four feet away into a banyan tree.

"Don't ever do that again," Artie had hissed in my ear, "or I'll kick your ass from here to Koko Head."

The old, one-legged man, after thinking about the offer and having been taken in by Artie's "true American hero" flattery, finally agreed, and gave Artie the handling and mailing fee in cash, which probably meant the poor guy couldn't eat for a week.

I wanted to bust Artie on the nose, and only restrained myself because, as I said, I loved being fed and housed in Makiki Heights.

As we were walking up the road from the old guy's house, we heard someone calling for us to come back. We turned and saw the old guy furiously hopping on his one leg trying to catch up to us.

He was scrawny and pathetic, bare-chested and bare-footed, wearing only a threadbare pair of khaki shorts.

"Hey, young fella," the old guy said. "I shouldn't have done that. I just remembered I got an electricity bill to pay. Can I get my money back?

Artie's instant answer came in the form of a verbal punch to the solar plexis. "fuck you," he spat and walked off.

I didn't have any money, or I would have gladly given it to the poor guy who was just left standing there on one foot, looking sad as hell in the hot Hawaiian sun.

After my three weeks training was complete, it was my turn to show my trainer what I could do.

The fact that this was a scam that bothered me, but I sincerely wanted to prove I could do this job as well as anyone else. In my private time, I had rehearsed and rehearsed my presentation. To myself, I sounded great, very persuasive. I was ready to take on the world.

One difference in their script and mine, was that I would inform the people I solicited—once I was out there on my own without Artie—that they could also buy the magazine in a store for less, but that the benefit of ordering it from me was that it would be delivered.

On a grimly hot morning, grimmer for the fact that Artie would be surveying my every move and every word, we set out. Our destination was a decidedly lower class neighborhood off Kapiolani Boulevard where people, seeing the lush pages of the Paradise of the Pacific Magazine, were apt to be hypnotized into a world they were otherwise barred from, the world of the wealthy and the beautiful.

The fact was, this magazine sold better with people who couldn't afford it than those who could. It had been shown, through research, that the people who could afford the magazine were already living the lifestyle of the rich and famous. So why did they need a magazine showing them doing the same exact thing?

Honolulu's really poor neighborhoods, then as now, were very depressing. The sun would beat down relentlessly on structures no better than hovels. Inside these hovels, all surfaces ran with cockroaches and palmetto bugs, some an inch or more long. It gave me the creeps just being there.

It was, in fact, a cockroach-infested apartment I'd taken in a neighborhood like this that had propelled me into seeking a sales job with the "Paradise of the Pacific Magazine" in the first place.

I'd taken that apartment in a similarly run-down neighborhood on King Street. It looked pretty bad in the daytime, but at night was 10 times worse. That's when the cockroaches would crawl out of every crevice in the place.

I had given the landlord a month's security deposit, a month's rent, and an extra month's security that he insisted upon. After a night of standing up mostly as the bugs went this way and that, I'd asked for a refund. It was refused.

There was no way I could keep the place which is when I heard about the magazine job, applied, and got it.

Having arrived in Honolulu several months before with nothing but a winter wardrobe and very little cash, I realized that I'd made a very rash decision to come here in the first place, especially without planning it out better. It wasn't long before I regretted having left San Francisco.

Gone was my job in the photographic unit of the Metropolitan Life Insurance Company. As for my apartment, I'd left it and all my worldly possessions in the hands of a friend, Carlotta, a failed Hollywood starlet turned Beatnik.

Carlotta was something of an intellectual, an avid reader, and fun to be with. We'd never been lovers, just friends. We spent many hours sitting at the bar at the Vesuvio Café in North Beach. When I mentioned to her that I was leaving for Hawai'i, she offered to apartment-sit during my time away.

I told her I didn't know how long that would be, and she said that was fine by her as she didn't have a place of her own.

What had caused my departure from San Francisco was the fact that Patty O'Rourke, the girl I was in love with, was marrying my rival, Terry Morrison. I was heartbroken. It was a choice of either jumping off the Golden Gate Bridge, or sailing under it.

I chose the latter.

On the very day of their wedding, and the very hour, I was aboard the USS President Cleveland staring up at the underside of that fabled Bridge as we headed out to sea.

Hawai'i would be a new start for me. My idea was to work in the great outdoors, and through someone who was the friend of someone else who was the friend of someone else who was a friend of my only contact in the islands, Alan Saperstein, I landed a job as a sprinkler installer.

I could have had a better job, perhaps as a desk clerk at the Royal Hawaiian Hotel, but it would have meant being sodomized by a headhunter I'd contacted who made it clear that that was the deal.

Being young and naïve, I wasn't that young and naïve when he hinted broadly as to what I would have to do in order to secure a better job.

So, telling him where he could go, I instead took the sprinkler job. The sprinkler people told me that they would teach me how to install sprinklers. It was on my first and only day with them, I realized this wasn't true. Instead of installing sprinklers, I would be digging the trenches into which the sprinkler pipes were to be buried.

"Believe me, you won't be doing no installing," a Filipino co-laborer told me. "I been with them twenny years, and I'm still digging ditches..."

This bit of information dampened my enthusiasm, but that wasn't the reason I only worked one day. It was something else—a nearly fatal sunburn.

Working shirtless and without the benefit of sun lotion, I may as well have jumped into a fiery cauldron. I did note how the mainly Samoan and Filipino crew were covered up with long-sleeved shirts and wide-brimmed hats. I was also aware of how they looked at me with a mixture of contempt and puzzlement as to how I could work so exposed to the sun. But that's as far as all warning signs went.

"That crazy haole," I heard one Samoan say to another. "His mama no give him brains..."

I didn't yet know that "haole" was a derogatory term meaning "dumb white man". In my case, a dumb white man was about to become a dumb bright red man. With third degree burns all over my torso, shoulders, arms, neck and head.

My only recourse, after recuperating as best as possible in my bug-infested apartment, was to take this job selling "Paradise of the Pacific Magazine" door to door.

The owners of the magazine were a married "haole" couple worth big bucks from their scam. They were cold and distant and never spoke to me. Nor was there much communication between me and any of the other trainees and trainers. We weren't there to socialize, but to learn the tricks of the trade and to bring in the money. A failure to do that meant being thrown out in the street.

After the three weeks training were up, the day of my initiation had arrived. Artie and I got into his car and drove to another impoverished neighborhood, this one off Beretania Street. He then stood beside me as I knocked on my very first door. Moments later, the lady of the house appeared. She had to be six feet, five inches tall, and 400 pounds.

"Whatchu want, haole?" She was wearing a muu-muu the size of auditorium drapes, and an expression of extreme annoyance.

"I said whatchu want, haole? You deaf in the head?" she barked. I looked up at her and then over to Artie and then back at her and back at Artie and back at her and back at Artie and back at her...

"Uh..."

"I'll ass you one more time," her voice thundered, "whatchu doin' comin' round here knockin' on my door and botherin' me?"

As if mesmerized by her fierce, angry expression and the flat, lines of her Polynesian warrior's face, I realized this was no job for me.

"...Oh, never mind," I said, as I walked away or, to be more accurate, tried to walk away.

'I quit," I told Artie. He had trained me for three weeks, and I was quitting on my very first try.

Artie, not willing to accept the defeat I so willingly accepted, spun me around and pushed me back toward the door. He then addressed the woman.

"Ma'am," he said, "this here is one sorry excuse for a trainee if I ever saw one. Please let me explain our fabulous offer to you so that you will have all the information which you are entitled to..."

"Listen, shithead," the woman responded, "if you don't get away from my house, I will turn my dogs on you. Now FUCK OFF!!!"

At that point, my life was in danger, not from the woman's dogs, but from this mad dog called Artie who was just about foaming at the mouth.

I turned my back on him and walked on. If I was going to be attacked, I would be attacked. Very surprisingly, all Artie did was fling a string of insults and threats at me.

It took me about an hour by foot to reach the gorgeous house up in Makiki Heights. Entering, I saw that lunch was being served to the new trainees. I would have loved to have helped myself at the buffet, but I knew I had to get out of the place quickly. Artie had obviously continued going the rounds in what was to be my territory and would be there soon.

Racing to my room, I threw my few possessions into my small suitcase and was out the door, having no idea where I would go, what I would do, or even if I would survive.

But I knew I'd made the right decision. This was no way to make a living.

Honolulu, in those days, wasn't anything like it is today. It was no melting pot. White folks and black folks were targets of hate. I had a hard time for a while, slept on beaches, did whatever day work I could get, scrounged for food, and eventually got a job at the Waldon Feed Mill on the Nimitz Highway.

Malnutrition and mononucleosis followed, and so my Hawaiian adventure was drawing to a close after just about eight months. I borrowed money from my dad and flew back to the safety of the apartment I had turned over to Carlotta, in San Francisco. Only Carlotta wasn't there.

When I'd gone off to Hawai`i, I had left a fair number of possessions such as clothes, a record player, a TV, a radio, books, furniture and all sorts of other things.

All of which Carlotta had, as I found out from the

Chinese family next door, sold. And there were two months rent in arrears.

But, there was an angel willing to help me, give me time to recover my health, get a job, and make all the back payments on the rent. She was my landlady, Mrs. Kathleen Kerr.

Mrs. Kerr was in her eighties, had lost a son in WWII, and said I reminded her of him.

Another reason she liked me, was because I told her quite often what a lovely Irish lass she was. I wasn't feeding her a line. At over 80, she had the twinkle in her eye of an 18 year old, and the smile to go with it.

And that was no blarney.

19

Tuneless yelping, groaning, screaming, and screeching. In other words: today's pop music.

Remember popular music the way it used to be? Those beautiful, intricate and elegant melodies that transported you to strange, enchanted places? The lyrics were poetic masterpieces that you could actually understand.

People's lives were richer because there were so many tunes you could sing in the shower or hum when at work. There were the great romance backdrop tunes that seemed to be written just for you: "In the Still of the Night", "I Concentrate on You", and "Stardust Melody".

There were the songs that instructed you to "Button Up Your Overcoat" and "Make Someone Happy".

And before the plethora of inspirational self-help books, there were inspirational self-help songs such as "Pick Yourself Up" and "Smile" and "Life is Just a Bowl of Cherries".

Today, so many pop music composers and lyricists seem to have forgotten the art of "transportation" in favor of tuneless, blaring, screaming, pockets of noise.

The death of the catchy melody is the worst of it. There aren't the intricacies of composition that were the earmarks of all the great composers who worked in this field from the turn of the 20th century and on, from Jerome Kern up through Stephen Sondheim.

Today, you might hear an artist with a truly magical talent for singing or musicianship involved in some vague dirge that, no matter how loud or how many embellishments that are tacked on, still sounds like some vague dirge, repeated over and over again, ramming itself into one's head until one's head wants to explode.

This trend may have started with the Beatles rendition of "Hey Jude" although it took 40 years to fully materialize.

It is said that each generation looks back on the previous generation's outpouring of music and rolls its collective eyes skyward.

But in years to come, what will future generations think of this generation's bland, feeble, and disposable output?

Who, in 50 years, will consider some of the material produced today as classics?

Music, like many of our art forms: Painting, literature, design, is in great jeopardy. Golden Oldies have avoided being encased in the amber of time, like so many prehistoric insects. It's still out there, but where are the Golden Oldies of the present time and the future?

The music of past generations, which gave tremendous pleasure to so many included the great standards such as "My Funny Valentine", "The Way You Look Tonight", "Moon River", "Blues in the Night", "Georgia," "Here's That Rainy Day", "Stardust Melody", "Long Ago and Far Away", "I'll Be Seeing You", "As Time Goes By", "Leaving on a Jet Plane", "I Want to Hold Your Hand", "I've Got You Under My Skin", "You're the Top", "A Foggy Day", "I Remember You",

"Boogie Woogie Bugle Boy from Company B", "I'm Old Fashioned", "Love is a Many-Splendored Thing", "The Theme from Titanic", "I Can't Get Started", "Pennies from Heaven", "But Not For Me", "Summertime", "A Fine Romance". "Isn't it Romantic", "Time After Time", "Brother, Can You Spare a Dime?", "Polka Dots and Moonbeams", "Out of Nowhere", "What a Difference a Day Made", "Dearly Beloved", "Sentimental Journey", "Laura", "The Look of Love", "I Say a Little Prayer", "Begin the Beguine", "Lullaby of Birdland", "Honeysuckle Rose", "I Get a Kick Out of You", "At last", "It's De-Lovely", "It Only Happens When I Dance With You", "I had the Craziest Dream", "Misty", "Beauty and the Beast", "You Took Advantage of Me", "How High the Moon", "I've Heard that Song Before"…just to name a bunch.

To really have a better idea of the way pop music has gone down the drain, just look at the tunes of past years compared to tunes of today that have been nominated for or have won Academy Awards.

So many of those tunes from years and years ago are still being sung today: "Over the Rainbow", "The Way You Look Tonight", "It Might as Well Be Spring", "Secret Love", "All the Way", "The Days of Wine and Roses", "Call Me Irresponsible", "The Shadow of Your Smile", "The Windmills of Your Mind", "Raindrops Keep Fallin' On My Head", "I've Had the Time of My Life", "The Way We Were"…

And even the Academy Award losers are on the repertoires of singers and musicians who keep those titles alive: "I've Got You Under My Skin", "They Can't Take That Away From Me", "Cheek to Cheek", "Blues in the Night", "Happiness is Just a Thing Called Joe", "That old Black Magic", "You'd Be So Nice to Come Home to", "I Can't Begin to Tell You", "It's Magic",

"That's Amore", "We Mustn't Say Goodbye", "Unchained Melody", "An Affair to Remember"…

In all honesty, when was the last time you whistled to the tune of "The Lord of the Rings: The Return of the King"?

What I am saying is not just my opinion. In talking to a number of young people, they have also expressed concerns. One person told me that the abundance of such bad pop music is a good thing because it will eventually create a situation where composers will be forced to come up with something far better.

Current singers themselves, such as Harry Connick, Jr., Diana Krall, and Michael Buble rely on the old standards because there are no new standards for them. Even Rod Stewart has switched from the raucous, rowdy music he became known for, and is putting out albums of oldies. To hear him sing "Long Ago and Far Away" is like, well, music to my ears.

Of course, there is a market for a lot of what's going on today. Just try to drive through town without your car (not to mention your body) starting to vibrate to some young kid's boom box to your left or right?

It's not Sinatra on that boom box. It's a rap artist thundering out 90 words a minute, or a heavy metal band attempting to assassinate your nerve endings.

Those perpetrators of such intrusive tones are playing with your future ability to actually "hear" music, or anything else, for that matter. Many people who've continuously listened to loud music are now hearing-impaired. Just observe how they talk louder than other people, as if it's you who is deaf.

But aside from anything else, there's nothing memorable about the sounds they are producing other than the splitting headache you can't shake.

Memory and music are a part of people's lives, And

they associate that music with important life events, such as a first love. What kind of music will future generations associate with their magic moments—"It's hard Out There to be a Pimp?"

20

Nannies who shouldn't be allowed near kids.

You might want to really check out the person into whose care you are entrusting your baby's well-being.

Chances are, a sterling resume won't tell the whole story. The sweet, nurturing-seeming babysitter, nurse, or governess might actually be anything but.

And who's to know? Babies can't talk.

When I was a young dad with two small boys I would, each lunchtime, leave the ad agency where I worked on East 53rd Street in Manhattan and walk the short distance to my apartment on East 57th Street.

There, I would relieve my wife of our two small sons, one of whom was just born, and the other who was 13 months older, get them into their big Rolls Royce of a carriage (a British Marmot), and wheel them back up Fifth Avenue, past the Plaza Hotel and over to Central Park.

A man pushing a big baby carriage was a strange sight in those days. Actually, I think I was the first dad in this category, thereby opening up a whole new frontier in which other dads were to follow without embarrassment.

Those were the days just before it became okay for dads to be seen as nurturers, instead of just breadwinners. In fact, it helped women change roles as well, as breadwinners instead of just nurturers.

I was a combination of both…a nurturer and breadwinner, and Central Park was a place where I exhibited the former. The park was then, as today, riddled with nannies. No matter where I chose to park the buggy, There they would be, of British, Irish or German extraction, their little charges nearby in equally large Marmots.

These nannies always regarded me suspiciously. They would make no attempt to cover up their rather frank appraisals of me. It was obvious what they were thinking: What was a grown man doing in their midst? I was speaking baby talk, no less.

But I didn't mind; I loved being a dad and these two little individuals gave me great joy as I goo-gooed and rocked them to sleep.

Probably, I was mistaken for some sort of male nanny being that I was usually in business attire. It didn't escape me that I was seen as a threat to the ancient female bastion of nannydom.

Another reason for their stand-offish behavior had to do with the fact that men had taken over almost every walk of life. Was this to be another area they would infiltrate and take over? Would female nannies soon become obsolete, lose their jobs and professions, be shipped back to spend the rest of their lives in the lonely bed-sitting rooms of Cheltenham or Slough or Limerick or Düsseldorf?

I would have happily entered a conversation with these gals, but they wanted no part if it, no part of me. A smile in their direction was met by deadly, beady eyes. They might not wish to converse with me, but they yakked nonstop with one another and I was privy to their conversations. One of which chilled me to the bone.

"Oh, vat I vouldn't giff for a little von like yours,

sleepink avay zo peazefully like an angel inztead of ziss von, a demandink little deffil if ever I zaw von," one nanny said to another.

"Vell, dearie," the other nanny said, "it's not a natural zleep, you know."

"Vhat do you mean not natural?" asked the first nanny.

"Just vat I said. I haff to put ze babe to zleep myself by zpecial meanz or I vill neffer get any peaze."

"Put the babe to zleep yourzelf? By zpecial meanz?"

"Dot's right. It's very zimple. I chust turn on ze gas uffen and hold little Timmy's head in zere for a full minute. I count zlowly back from zixty. Zometimes from von hundred and tventy ven he's been ezpecially cantankerous. Verks vonnnnders."

"Zo you gazzz the little brat?"

"Oh I vouldn't call it gazzz...not like za fuhrer vould do, God blezz hiz zoal...it's like a zleeping pill."

Sitting there, privvy to this this conversation, I couldn't believe my ears. Two Nazi nannies decades after za fuhrer was dead, discussing the use of a gas oven as a solution, though not a final solution, for their wards.

Right then and there I knew I had to do something about it. But what? Could I call the cops? The FBI? Could I follow them back to where they worked and report to their employers what I'd heard? Who would believe me? If it sounded unbelievable to me, it would do so to everybody else.

There was no possibility of my doing anything about this at this point. No time. I had to drop off the boys at home and then get back to work, but I couldn't shake off what I'd heard.

About a week after this incident with the Nazi

Nannies, my wife was called home to Scotland where her father was seriously ill. She would be away for at least a week. I would have to find some help because it was going to be a very busy week of work and presentations at the agency.

I had plenty of relatives who were scattered across the five boroughs of New York City. I thought of calling any number of them to help me, but honestly, I think Gas Chamber Mary, a name I'd ascribed to the nanny in the park, would have been preferable.

There was a time when we'd hired someone from an agency, a Mrs. Parkson, a grandmotherly type who looked reliable, nurturing, and more than competent. We left our beautiful babies with her and traveled less than a mile for a weekend at the Plaza Hotel. It was to be a weekend of relaxation and fun.

"I'm just going to call Mrs. Parkson to see how everything is going," my wife suggested on the afternoon of our first day away.

"The older one is wandering from room to room calling for you. They won't eat, they won't sleep, and by the way, the one who's teething? He's chewing on an electric cord."

My wife and I were checked out of the Plaza, into a cab, and home in ten minutes flat.

So who was I to hire? After what I'd heard in Central Park, I was damned if I would hire some strange woman to watch the babies. She might be the sister of the Gas Chamber Mary for all I knew.

Sometimes, I would, when my wife had an appointment somewhere, take the babies to work. I loved my job, my agency, my co-workers, and the secretaries loved watching the boys if I was in a client meeting or something.

It wasn't unusual for me, at times, to be burping

one or the other on my shoulder while working with an art director.

To do this for a full week was out of the question. I decided that, even though a big presentation was coming up in which I was key, they'd have to do it without me. Rather than risk my children's lives, I would have to risk the wrath of my boss and stay home with the kiddies.

I had some vacation time and took it, thereby becoming a full- time dad.

This was going to be quite an adventure for the three of us, because, aside from our Central Park jaunts, I usually only saw my sons a short time in the morning and for a short time before their evening bedtime.

And as it turned out, being at work would have been a vacation compared to the week I spent caring for my kids. They both came down with colds, cried a lot, were cranky and regarded me as a poor substitute for their lovely mom, their little eyes seeming to resent my very existence.

It was as if they were saying: "Who are you? Get out of here! There's only one person in our lives who matters. And it isn't you! We want our mother!"

I checked them out. There was no diaper rash, no diaper pins sticking them. But the crying persisted.

Panicking, I took them to our pediatrician to see if there was anything wrong with them, and thankfully, after a thorough exam, there wasn't. Their colds were making them impossible to live with.

They weren't the only ones missing their mom. By day three, I was ready for the loony bin. First I would pick up one baby and try to sooth him, and then I would pick up the second baby and try to sooth him, too. Then I would pick them up at the same time and try to sooth them both. I couldn't fool them. I was not their mother and their continual crying told me so.

Sleep was out of the question for me; I camped out on a chair in their room every night and would be on my feet the minute I heard either of them needing my attention.

The fact is, I was always terrified of the possibility of crib death. So from the time they were born, I would, several times a night, go into their rooms and place my hand on their shoulders to make sure they were breathing.

I feel foolish admitting this, but I would go into their rooms and do the same thing even when they were 13 and 14 years old. That's the kind of father I was.

By day three, their colds had abated, but their tempers hadn't. Now they were just plain angry. Their cries even had a certain cadence: "WE WANT OUR MOM, WE WANT OUR MOM. WE WANT OUR MOM!!!"

By day six, they were well enough to be taken out in their carriage. Over to Central Park we would go. It was a mild December as I recall. The nannies hadn't seen me, their male arch enemy, for a week and here I was again.

Even if they wanted to ignore me, which they obviously did, they couldn't ignore the cries of my two sons. Finally, Gas Chamber Mary got up and approached me.

Vat a disssaster," she said, her German lilt lilting, "chust look at zese poor dear little anchels."

A chill went through me as she bent down and nuzzled them under their chins. Miraculously, they abruptly stopped crying. I looked at them. They weren't looking at me. They were looking at her. Now they were smiling up at her.

Then the nanny gave me some advice. "Should zey start cryink at home, zere iss a vay to stop zat. Vat I do is tie a long piece of strink around their little pinkies...and ven they start their cryink, I chust YANK it hard, and zey stop cryink. It doesn't happen at first. You have to keep doink it. Zen, von day, the little beggerz learn that iff zey cry, zey gets za "treatment".

Hearing this, and thinking about the gas oven atrocity, it all came to a head and I finally, angrily, spoke up, "And do you also YANK out their fingernails while you are at it? Is that something you learned in the Gestapo?"

The advice from this harridan came to an abrupt halt. Her eyes widened and her back stiffened. She immediately got up, and without looking in my direction, grabbed the baby carriage of her charge and departed. The last I saw of her, she was scurrying down a path, no doubt as horrified by my comment as I had been of hers. And then the babies started to howl again.

That nanny's methods for getting the silence Gas Chamber Mary so favored stayed in the forefront of my mind all the way home. I thought of those poor, innocent little babies that were being so abused. It was appalling. I resolved that I would seek out the employers of these women to expose their horrendous practices just as soon as I could.

I would also get in touch with the nanny-hiring employment places and alert them to the dangerous and unscrupulous practices of some of the women they sent out.

And I would also write a letter to the editor of the New York Times to bring about awareness of the problem. These women had to be stopped!

But I have to admit that I, as I wheeled my constantly wailing little twosome home, my mind kept wandering back to the string idea.

21

Birthday cards that announce your exact age.

One of the best kept secrets that exists today is how old you are. This is a well-guarded bit of information that no one has been able to coax out of you.

People in your social group are dying off due to old age. There are just a few left who know your exact birth date for sure.

And you are comforted by the thought that even they won't be around very much longer.

But then, you receive a birthday card with your exact age plastered all over it. Not the age you have allowed people to think you are, but the actual ghastly one.

How did the sender even find out?

Probably everyone knows by now, God forbid.

You will not display this card amongst all your other birthday cards so others will see it, that's for sure. But you've seen it, and that's more than enough to ruin your day.

Who are these people who send you such painful reminders? What are they trying to accomplish? Those large digits in red dominate the front of the card. Do they think for even one minute that you don't know your own age?

Either these so-called well-wishers are unconscious or sadistic or both.

Maybe they're just young. Young people tend to think that growing old is reserved for old people.

Whatever the case, a card that congratulates you on becoming old and decrepit isn't very becoming.

Age-related messages are some of the most popular in the greeting card field. And they are perfectly permissible when a person is six years old.

For the much older person, however, they should be banned. Which is not to say that they aren't extremely funny and clever. If you go to a card shop and look at all the age-related cards, you can get quite a few laughs.

Hilarious as they may be to a younger audience, they are rarely funny or clever to someone who is old, wrinkled, and ready to kick the bucket.

The sender may laugh heartily, but the recipient will hardly be joining in.

Having reached an age when I don't feel the rush of youthful ambition, it's a pleasure to do the things I prefer, which doesn't necessarily mean I am ready to throw in the towel.

Yes, it's true that getting on in years might mean the loss of certain aids to a carefree life, such as one's memory or teeth, but these are replaced with a certain peace of mind that only comes with age.

You can interview anyone of a certain vintage, asking if they would ever want to be young again. Many will say absolutely not. Others might say, only if they knew what they know now.

Youth has its disadvantages, such as not really knowing what is important in life and thinking that bright, bushy-eyed health and vitality are endless; that being 22 is forever.

Getting on in years doesn't mean a person is without merit, even though society tends to ignore older people while making a big deal out of young people. It's kind of funny in a way, because the younger the achiever, the more accolades.

Shouldn't it be the other way around? That the older the achiever, the more accolades?

Actually, there are ceremonies celebrating the achievements of older people. They're called life achievement awards and implicit in the giving of each award is the message: Thank you. You have now done your life's work and your life is now over.

I'm an older person, and I have a very busy schedule because I'm a publisher and I also run a non-profit organization and I also write books. These are just some of my pastimes…and yet, a young person will come up to me and ask me: "Are you retired?"

Retaining my calm although wanting to wrap this question around the young person's impertinent neck, my usual reply is that I am not retired but that I dye my hair white!

We all get old unless something occurs to prevent that from happening.

Such as a fatal illness

Or a fatal accident.

Or how about a grisly murder by shooting, stabbing, strangulation, poisoning, or setting someone on fire.

As carried out on an obnoxious young card giver by a deranged, vengeance-seeking older, much older, senior citizen…

22

Not getting quarterly reports telling you what your taxes are paying for.

You go into a department store and buy something, and you get an itemized receipt. You order something online and you get an itemized receipt. In all your transactions you get a receipt that tells you what you paid for.

But with the government, you hand over your hard-earned cash and do you have any idea what you might have bought?

Maybe it's helping to pay for a tank that will go out and kill people.

Maybe it's paying for some congressman's vacation in the Bahamas.

You never know.

Wherever your money has gone, you have had no proposal from the government as to where the money is going to be allotted, no opportunity to approve or disapprove, no voice in the matter, nothing.

You get a few inklings when you vote. You can approve or disapprove the measures presented to you, but those measures are a tiny sprinkling as to how our money is spent.

For example, has there ever been a ballot asking you if you supported the war in Iraq?

We have congressmen who are supposed to carry

out what their constituencies want to see happen, but has your congressman ever sent you a letter asking you what you want to see happen?

Or if you agree on any of the government spending?

Those of us who pay taxes (in other words, all of us), are kept in the dark.

You no doubt have ideas on how our tax money is spent. Perhaps you'd rather that we liberate the poverty-stricken people of West Virginia than the people of Afghanistan.

Or maybe you'd rather we spent some money on raising teacher's salaries instead of buying new fighter planes that will be obsolete this time next year.

Whatever it is that the people of this country would like to see, where is the arena to express those ideas?

I'm not against paying taxes if they are for the upkeep of our country. It's a privilege to pay them just as it is a privilege to live here.

It would be nice, however, to have a say in how the money is spent. I resent how the IRS comes on like the Gestapo, especially when we are financing a war or two.

Through the centuries since this country has existed, we have been threatened by foreign powers. Within living memory, communism was the big deal. On the whim of just a few men in Washington, starting with Harry S. Truman, we were determined to curtail the spread of this ideology. We invaded lands where we were not wanted and watched as hordes of people, on both sides, died in Korea and Vietnam.

Their deaths did nothing to end communism. Those were just lives thrown away. Ironically, capitalism now appeals to Russia and China.

So perhaps our war against any current power not

in accord with us is a similar, futile struggle.

Whether we spend our taxes on such negative endeavors as war, or in promoting life and well-being on our planet, the decision should be up to us.

And each tax-paying citizen should have a quarterly report on his or her purchases.

Do you know how many people you may have inadvertently blown to bits today because of your tax dollars?

23

Close friends you think you know better than yourself.
Until you go on a trip with them.

If you want to keep your friends, keep your distance. Under no circumstances, go on a long trip with them.

I made a big mistake a couple of years ago when I went along with an idea suggested by a close friend of mine, Bill Buntley.

"Hey, why don't you join Sandy and me on a trip to Paris," Bill had said. "Just think, the Eiffel Tower, the Follies Bergere, all that great food".

Sandy was his wife. I'd only met her once briefly. I loved Bill's first wife, Kate, but I didn't know Sandy at all. Had I known her even a little, I never would have gone on this trip.

Bill had been a friend for years, ever since college when we shared a bachelor pad, friends, neckties...

When I married Betty, Bill was my best man. When Bill married Kate, I was his. And I would have been his best man when he married Sandy, but she made it plain that she didn't feel comfortable having the man who was the best man in Bill's first marriage as best man in the second. I understood, sort of.

More recently, I had lost Betty, and Bill was there

for me. When he'd had a cancer scare the following year, the role was reversed.

So when Bill's brainchild came up, it sounded terrific. And if there was anyone to go to Paris with, it was Bill. He was adventurous, fun, funny, positive. His sense of humor was that kind where you couldn't breathe because you were laughing so hard.

We had travel plans that included more than Paris. We would also go to Switzerland. And since we would be in Europe, Bill and I would fly to Scotland from Zurich and travel down Great Britain to London.

Sandy was invited to join us in the United Kingdom, but she said she would want to get home to the kids.

I made the air, hotel and car arrangements for our British jaunt, putting everything on my credit card. I figured we would split expenses at some point, but all that could wait. I also had my travel agent make the reservations for the Paris hotel for which we would all pay separately.

A week before the trip, Bill called me to say that his newly-divorced sister, Cecilia, was interested in joining us. I'd never met her, but any sister of Bill's had to be just as great as he was.

It would be a foursome rather than a threesome. It did cross my mind that Cecilia's inclusion might develop into something other than just traveling partners, which I wasn't even remotely ready for. It hadn't been that long before my beloved Betty had died, and I was still in a state of grief.

Finally, the departure day arrived. Bill, Sandy, and Cecilia flew down from Oregon to meet me for the flight from San Francisco. We were all psyched. Paris! I had been many times, and loved the city. I had also worked there quite a bit, so knew it thoroughly. I could show the others around. Neither Sandy nor Cecilia had ever been, and Bill only once.

Bill's birthday would be the same day as our arrival, and he announced that he was going to take us all out to the best restaurant in Paris.

We boarded the plane. Bill and Sandy sat in the seats in front of us, Cecilia and I next to each other. We chatted excitedly about all we were going to do once we landed.

At first I didn't mind that Cecilia was so attentive to me, but then I had a slightly apprehensive feeling about the way she was acting, which is to say she acted as if we were a couple. Some of the things she did struck me as a bit presumptuous. For example, she would cozy up to me as we watched the in-flight movie, take my hand now and then, and laugh at every joke that I made (even the ones that weren't funny), things like that.

By the time we reached Paris, anyone spotting us would have thought we were two couples, instead of one couple, one best friend, and one sister, separate and distinct. Cecilia walked with her arm in mine. I stiffly allowed this and all the advances she made until I had to put an end to it.

"Hey, Cecilia, we don't even know each other. Let's just be friends, okay?" That didn't stop her.

Why she was so forward, I can only conjecture. In putting together the pieces, I have a mental scenario of what might have occurred amongst the three of them back in Oregon.

There they would be, sitting around. Bill would mention Paris. He would mention that he and Sandy and I were going. Then Cecilia would have chipped in. "Can I go, too?"

And then they would have said, "sure...and Charlie's a widower…and single…maybe you and he could get together…"

Whatever had been said amongst them, for Cecilia, there seemed to be some kind of plan in mind.

We finally landed in Paris and we taxied to our hotel. It turned out that I was the only one who'd gone to the money exchange at home before leaving, and so paid the exorbitant taxi fare. It was just the first of many I would pay, because as the trip wore on, no one ever seemed to have any euros on them.

I should mention here that in business, Bill had far eclipsed me and was a millionaire many times over. I was comfortable, but not at all in his league.

But who was counting the money I was laying out? This was Bill, I was dealing with. Bill, my good friend. It would all be reckoned later. Or so I thought.

The hotel I had chosen, the Residence Foch, was small and exquisite. Each room was decorated with taste and imagination. We had fun choosing which rooms we would all be in. Bill and Sandy laid claim to the best. And Cecilia suggested that, to save money, we share a room. With all the tact I could muster, I quelled that notion.

To celebrate Bill's birthday, we wanted to go to the Tour d'Argent and couldn't get in on such short notice. The very nice desk clerk suggested Fellini on the Rue de l'Arbre. We excitedly took off for the restaurant in the taxi I paid for.

The restaurant and the dinner were flawless. What wasn't flawless was the mood Sandy had suddenly gotten into. She was sullen and complaining, and staring at me with daggers in her eyes. I had no idea why. She had drunk a prodigious amount of champagne.

We finished our coffee, and it was time to pay. Bill looked like he was going to have a heart attack. "I had no idea it would be this expensive," he said, looking at the bill; it was expensive: $700.00; so I split it with him.

Then out of nowhere, Sandy suddenly stood up and pointed a finger at me. In the dim light of the restaurant, she looked like a demented Meryl Streep.

"You've been taking advantage of Cecilia!" she shouted, causing other diners to turn around. "You've been playing a game with her, and I won't stand for it!"

I was taking advantage of Cecilia? Was she joking? I had done everything possible to dissuade Cecilia from making any more advances. Not only was I not attracted to her, but I didn't even like her.

I looked at Bill who only wore a kind of silly grin on his face; and at Cecilia who seemed mesmerized by what Sandy was saying.

Stunned by this sudden attack, I said I needed some air and walked out of the restaurant, trying to consider what to do. Which is when Sandy came storming after me.

"Don't you dare walk out without an explanation!" she said loudly. She was like a giant mosquito on my back ready to sting. To escape, I jumped into a taxi and headed back to the hotel. Three hours later, there was a knock on my door. I opened it a crack.

"I've come to apologize," Sandy said. She was in a nightgown and her hair was disheveled.

"Forget it," I said. "Go back to sleep."

"I can't forget it," Sandy said pushing the door open and entering the room. "I HAVE TO APOLOGIZE!"

"Your apology is accepted. Now why don't you go back to your room? We'll talk about it some other time," I said.

"WE WILL DISCUSS IT NOW!"

And so she stayed for over an hour, complaining about her life, about how Bill worked such long hours; how she was left with the children all day; how she had been looking forward to this trip; how she had now completely destroyed it.

I kept wondering where the hell Bill was. Why hadn't he come to collect his wife and get her out of my hair? No doubt he was fast asleep, and I was stuck with this madwoman.

Finally, and only because she was falling asleep, I was able to escort her, in our night clothes, up the stairs to her room. As she opened the door to go in, I could hear Bill snoring loudly.

Ah, sleep. Finally. But not for long. At promptly six in the morning, the garbage men came down our street. After a cacophony of garbage pails and lids that seemed to last forever, they were gone, to be replaced by cars being driven as only the French drive, noisily with shifting gears and honking horns.

But I didn't mind it. This was Paris. People here were alive, noisy, full of life.

Eventually however, with the thought that sleep would not be an option any longer, and with prospects for a fabulous day in Paris, I got out of bed, shaved, showered, dressed, and decided I would go down to breakfast. Probably the others were still asleep and I could have some private time over the traditional French breakfast of baguette and coffee.

What I saw when I reached the lobby had me rooted in my steps. Bill, Sandy, and Cecilia were checking out!

That's when Bill spotted me.

"I was just coming up to get you," he said. "Pack your things. We're getting out of here. We can't deal with the street noise. How in the world you could have booked us in a place like this is beyond me."

"You liked the place yesterday," I said.

"That was yesterday. This is today. We've made reservations for all of us on the Rue de Rivoli."

Bill's critical tone didn't sound like him. It sounded like Sandy. It was as if he was her spokesman, her puppet.

"Well, you guys go ahead. I like this hotel."

"You're kidding, right?" Bill said. "You're gonna stay in this dump?"

Meanwhile, Sandy was challenging the desk clerk in a voice loud enough to rival the noise of the garbage collectors. The desk clerk, by comparison, was calm and centered.

"You have made a reservation for a week, madam. You are therefore responsible for full payment,"

"The hell we are," Sandy stormed back. "We had no idea our rooms were practically in the street!"

"This is Paris, madam. There is traffic. There is noise. What did you expect?"

"Peace and quiet. Which is why we're getting the hell out of here. We'll pay for one lousy night and one night only. Take it or leave it.

Witnessing this, I could well understand why the French are said to hate Americans.

Meanwhile, I had Bill to contend with. "Now listen, Charlie. We came over here, the four of us, to be together, and we're going to stick together. Now go get your stuff."

This was my second mistake of the trip. Instead of letting the others go off without me, I obeyed. I went up to my room, quickly packed, came back down, apologized to the desk clerk/hotel owner and paid my bill.

The three I was traveling were waiting outside with a taxi loaded up. We headed off for the other hotel. I paid for the taxi.

The new hotel was twice as expensive as the other hotel and had none of the charm. And if the other hotel was noisy, this new one was ear-shattering. But, again, I didn't mind. This was Paris. It was noisy. I loved it, even in the early morning hours.

As the Rodgers and Hart song goes: "I dodged the same old taxi cabs that I had dodged for years. The chorus of their squeaky horns was music to my ears..."

Bill, Sandy, and Cecilia still weren't happy. They changed their rooms twice and still weren't satisfied. They were finally situated in the back of the hotel away from the busy Rue de Rivoli and complained that there was no view.

I pointed out that they wouldn't be in the room all that much and that they wouldn't be needing a view, so they were appeased somewhat. It felt like the worst had occurred and now at last we could do all the things we wanted. Except that what Sandy, Bill, and Cecilia wanted was different from what I wanted. They preferred to spend their entire days in the hotel spa. They would emerge for meals, but that was it.

Trying to get them over to the Louvre, a five minute walk from the hotel, was nearly impossible. They had never been, and as Sandy had explained: "Seen one museum and you've seen them all. I happen to have been to eight museums in my life and so I consider myself quite up on art."

Being a person who has virtually lived in museums since a teenager, I kept up my campaign to get them to the Louvre, and finally, on the museum's late night, after the spa closed, they agreed to go. We had only been there a half-hour when the three of them suggested we get out of there and go for a drink.

"We only went for you," Bill generously offered.

On the street, I stumbled in a pothole and came crashing down on my left knee which was badly bruised and bloody, making it hard to walk.

None of my companions said anything much that would have been construed as supportive, but when I lifted my trouser leg to dab the blood away with a handkerchief, Cecilia whistled. "Hey, nice leg!" she exclaimed. Even then, it was all about sex.

"You'll live," nurse Sandy Ratchett dryly observed.

A couple more days in Paris and my knee was still painful. Plus, I was having chest pains. The stress of being with these people was getting to me. I didn't even recognize Bill at this point, so controlled was he by Sandy. All this led to one disagreement after another.

For example, I balked at being the one always paying for taxis and for chilled bottled water and in a number of cases, restaurant tabs.

"You're in a lousy mood," Bill would counter.

Leaving them one evening, I limped off on my own, thoroughly enjoyed dinner and people-watching and the wonderful Paris atmosphere in general.

Returning to the hotel, I bumped into Bill who was not at all friendly. There was none of the camaraderie of former days. He, in fact, seemed angry with me.

"Sandy says you're a hypochondriac. You've been complaining about your knee and your chest pains and all the rest of it...so you fell on your knee, so what? And those chest pains? Imaginary."

It was at this point, I decided that there was absolutely no reason for me to further travel with the three of them. We were to leave the next day and take the train to Switzerland. Going to bed that night, I thought how ridiculous it was to be in such a horrendous situation in such a fabulous part of the world.

I was resolved to curtail my participation. I would join the others for breakfast in the morning and say goodbye. I sighed a sigh of relief and turned off the light and went to sleep.

Why is it that everything looks different in pure daylight? At breakfast the next morning, Sandy and Bill were warm and considerate, and Cecilia wasn't her usual vampire self.

"We'll take the train to Interlaken, Switzerland, where we'll spend a day and night, and then we'll be off to Murren in the Alps...it's up about 10,000 feet. It's going to be so wonderful!"

"I won't be going," I said. "I'm not really feeling up to it. I'll spend a few more days in Paris and then fly to Edinburgh and meet you there at the end of next week, Bill." My thought was that maybe by then Bill would be back to his usual, great self, without Sandy.

"There he goes again," Sandy sighed, "Mr. Temperamental."

"So you're going to abandon us," Bill said. "You're going to wreck our trip by being petulant. Don't you know that we love you? So what if we've had spats... that's what people who are close to one another do. They fight. They are passionate. Don't be so immature, Charlie. We need you. We need you to be with us."

You would have thought I'd have learned by this time. But I hadn't. Like a good little boy, I agreed to go to Switzerland with them when all I wanted to do was to get as far away as possible from them.

We took the train to Interlaken, that afternoon. The train trip was coldly congenial. I wondered what I was doing there. In Interlaken, we stayed at the Metropole, but didn't see much of each other because they were in the spa the whole time. We agreed to meet at the train station for the trip to Murren.

I got to the train station on time; waited, and then when they didn't turn up, took off on my own. I figured they would be on the next train.

I finally got to Murren via a tram that climbed 10,000 feet up the white peaks of the Alps. This little town, with Jungfrau close up and majestic, was enchanting.

The hotel had been booked by Sandy, the one effort she made regarding travel plans. My room was said, by the kindly woman who welcomed me, to be the most sought-after by her clients. And I could see why. It had a panoramic view of the Alps which left you breathless.

I unpacked, gazed at my own private view for a long while, and then, as evening approached and with no sign of the other three, had a long walk in this fairyland. Returning, I went into the lounge where I played the piano for an hour.

Looking up from the piano as someone approached, I saw it was Bill. I started to greet him but got cut off.

"You stole our room," he said.

"I what?"

"Sandy reserved that room for us, and you stole it."

"You're kidding, right?" I asked.

"We get here, and what do we find? Your crap in our room."

"Hey, hold on. It was the room they gave me. I didn't know you wanted it. Don't worry. "I'll have them give me another room and move my stuff there."

"We already did," Bill said.

"You already did what?" I asked.

"We moved your stuff…"

"You what?"

"We moved your stuff…and we had the maids

remake our bed and change the towels and scrub the toilet."

I might have argued about this with Bill, pointing out that a violation had been perpetrated in them touching my things, but Bill wasn't Bill anymore. He was Sandy. The Bill I knew was dead. So, I was afraid, was our friendship.

"You mean you didn't have them repaint the walls? Or put in new carpeting?" I said, walking off to find out where my new room was located.

I was sitting in the new room reading when I heard the three of them pass my door. They were apparently going to dinner without asking me if I wanted to join them. I can't say the solitary dinner I had at a nearby restaurant wasn't enjoyable. But this trip had turned into one nightmare after another.

Back at the hotel, I saw the three sitting in the lounge and tried to walk past them unseen. That didn't work.

"I'm sick of your mood," I heard Bill say. "So you can forget the trip to the U.K."

"My mood?"

"Yeah, your mood. You've been sulking and sour-faced this entire trip. Having you along with us was a big mistake."

"Uh huh," I said, going to my room. Out of the corner of my eye, I saw Sandy who was glaring at me. For what, I didn't know, or care.

The next morning, the three of my companions had gone off somewhere without telling me what they were planning for the day. I was just as glad. I had one last walk around this wondrous place, but to be honest, I just didn't see the beauty. I just wanted to get away from there as soon as possible.

I packed my bag, checked out of the hotel, and

made my way to the cable car and took it down, this being the first leg of a journey on my way to Zurich. I had one burning desire, to forget about traveling to Scotland and England, to get the hell out of Europe altogether, and to get back to my home in California. But could I get a flight?

Arriving at a nearly deserted airport hours later (most flights leave in the morning), I was in despair. The ticket counters all looked empty. But then I saw someone.

There was a woman just finishing up the day's work. She spoke English and was able to get me onto a flight leaving the next morning. It was going to cost me a lot of money for this new ticket. I couldn't change the old one, but I didn't care. I just wanted out of Europe

About a month later, Sandy emailed me. Bill was deeply depressed because I hadn't been in contact. Was I angry with them?

I emailed back that I wasn't angry, had taken responsibility for going on a trip with them, and that, incidentally, I had had to pay for the cancellation of the UK trip and there was a penalty for the cancellation of the first hotel in Paris, plus that I paid the travel agent fee and that they owed me $1600.

I never heard from either Sandy or Bill again.

As for my knee injury, that took another six months to heal. And the heart pain I felt in Paris? It was due to a clogged artery. A week after returning from Europe, I was rushed to the hospital where an angioplasty procedure took place.

So once again, I caution people who have the good fortune of caring friends. See them for lunch or dinner, but nothing more than that.

Even overnight can be dangerous.

24

For men: You've taken a woman out for dinner and want to impress her.

And then the waiter gives her the bill.

No tip for that guy. What his action has signified is that you are a eunuch.

Not capable of paying.

A loser.

Invisible.

And all the other crappy things you've ever thought about yourself.

Or maybe from the waiter's point of view, your date appears to have more testosterone than you do, more power and clout.

The waiter has destroyed the night. Whether he did it consciously or unconsciously is besides the point. From the vibes you are giving off, he has probably decided that this woman couldn't possibly be interested in you.

So, in the end, it's your vibes that have caused him to make this social faux pas…and therefore, your fault.

Face it, buddy, you hardly qualify for this woman's boyfriend, but you do fit the category as this woman's girlfriend.

Total humiliation, something you may never get over. This is only part of what you are feeling. Anger is that other strong emotion. And not just at the waiter. The damn maitre d' has also been flirting with your date, right in front of you. And it hasn't escaped your noticing that she wasn't doing anything to dissuade him.

The fact that he is eight times more handsome than you, and years younger, is more than evident.

You reach over with a sickly smile and retrieve the bill, painfully aware that the woman is perceiving you. She's perceiving like crazy, as if saying that if you were a real man, that this never would have happened.

A major clue to how she is feeling is her quickly turned cheek when you reach over and try to kiss here. Those latch-bolted lips of hers confirms this.

It occurs to you that she's shallow, undeserving of you, someone you're lucky to be rid of.

But damn, you were looking forward to some amorous moments after dinner.

Wait! Maybe not all is lost. You've settled the bill and have left the waiter with a 20 cent tip instead of a 20% tip, and with the superior smile of the customer who has wreaked his revenge, you don't even acknowledge him as you depart the restaurant.

It's then that you try to salvage the night. You suggest having a drink at the bar across the street. But she tries to beg off saying she has to write a report before she goes to sleep and that she has to be up for an early morning meeting.

You look at your watch and tell her it's only 9:30p.m. and you'll let her go after just one drink.

"Just one," she says.

You might have had a glass of Chardonnay at dinner, but now you order a series of boilermakers.

Throwing them down one after another, you are aware that this woman is now looking at you with renewed interest.

The expression on her face changes from that of disinterested to "hey, maybe there's something here, after all..."

You are, in her eyes, a hard drinker, hard liver, and all around hard character.

She allows you to move your bar stool closer to hers. And she allows you to take her hand. She then responds to your romantic gestures just as you'd hoped. You give her the supreme kiss. Not just a peck and pull away, but the long, soulful, passionate version.

Her "just one" drink limit has given way to a second drink. And a third. And fourth.

And that first kiss has given way to a second, third and fourth as well.

The two of you are so hot now, that there seems to be only one destination after this. You've only to decide your place or hers.

Which is when the bartender arrives with the bill.

And gives it to *her*.

25

Buying the expensive wedding gift for that sweet young couple that you know is going to divorce in less than a year.

There should be a revised etiquette about giving wedding gifts. The rule should be: No wedding gifts before the couple has completed one year of marriage. Make that 5 years. No, 10. How about until one or the other dies?

It has long been my belief that some couples only get married for the gifts including the huge check that the parents of the bride give the couple and the down payment on a house from the parents of the groom.

With the divorce rate as it is, isn't it a waste of money giving a gift until you know these people are going to stick together? For that matter when you consider the travel expenses, new outfit to wear, and the wear and tear on you, is it even worth going to the wedding?

If they can't make a commitment, why should you?

And what about the parents that bankrupt themselves to give their kids great weddings? They should have a contract drawn up which states that if the couple breaks up, every single penny will be returned, plus interest.

I had a friend who was the marrying kind. When he married for the first time, I blew my entire paycheck on cut-glass finger bowls from Tiffany's.

He didn't stay in that marriage long. The finger bowls went to the wife, otherwise I would have asked for them back.

Then he married a second time. Same thing. A very expensive gift. Big, fluffy monogrammed towels.

I may as well have had them monogrammed his and his, because that marriage went on the rocks as well.

There were two more times, and quite honestly, I wasn't as generous on those occasions as I had been previously. It was chopstick service for 12, genuine plastic. And as for the last gift, it was a plastic again...a salad bowl in day-glo orange that I'd got in a 99 cents store.

Funny thing about that salad bowl. It is used each time I'm invited to dinner by my friend and his wife.

At first, I thought it was being used because my friend and his wife wanted me to know how much they liked and appreciated it.

But no, in time I got to recognize the rather sinister look on my friend's face when he forced the salad bowl on me.

"Have some salad from this really classy bowl you gave us when we got married," he would say.

"I've decided that if they stay married for 60 years, I'll replace the plastic bowl with glass of some kind.

Another irritating aspect of giving presents is the lack of a thank you card in return.

A couple of years ago, I was called upon to perform a wedding for a very nice young couple.

As the person officiating at the wedding, there was no need for me to give the young couple a gift, but I liked them and gave them a check for $50.00.

According to all those authorities on such matters, it appears they all say the same thing about thank you note etiquette, the married couple has a year to respond.

But two years? Three years? Never? This was the case with the couple to whom I gave the check for $50.00.

Then, one day, I noticed the bride was working as a teller in a bank. I got in line and when it was my turn, I greeted her. I noticed a promotion being offered for something with a savings of $50.00.

"Oh, look at that," I said. "Very interesting. Fifty dollars...a nice number, that..."

If this connected with the young woman, I will never know. Her facial expression betrayed nothing.

And yup, I learned shortly after that she and her husband had indeed divorced.

I wanted my 50 bucks back.

But okay, this is life. Some people are conscious and some aren't. There were no thanks for this gift, or a great many of the other gifts I've given through the years.

It is said that a person who gives something to another person is not supposed to expect anything in return.

Excuse me, but that's bullshit.

26

Families in which you are a nobody unless you are a somebody.

The less successful you are, the more your own family is apt to compare you with other family members who are doing great.

Even if you become successful in some field or other, it might not matter. You will have already been branded. You can become the President of the United States and in the eyes of your family, you may never shine.

It was the October before last. I'd gone to New York to attend a wedding and while there, my extremely successful nephew, Reggie, and I decided to have lunch.

The fact that Reggie is considered one of the financial world's top whiz kids differs vastly from my own, far more humble, position in life. I'm not unsuccessful in what I do—in fact, I've done alright—but I'm not even remotely in Reggie's league. And on top of that, he's not even 40!

The major difference between us is that he operates from what appears to be the conservative and pragmatic resources of his left brain, while I stumble through each day, hardly able to balance my checkbook, and rarely straying from the more fertile, creative interior of my right brain.

You can see the problem. We don't have anything in

common, not a thing. Conversation between us doesn't come easily. An hour in each other's company can be torture, especially for him when he could be making another million dollars instead of being with me.

Anyway, on the day we were having lunch, I arrived at Reggie's Wall Street offices which were perched high up in an all-glass skyscraper that overlooked the entire world.

I knew it was going to be an effort getting through this lunch, and that it was probably one big mistake. What was I going to say to him? That when he was a kid, the family predicted that one day he would own the earth? And that their predictions came true?

Their predictions for me? Well, I'd rather not say—except that if they had come true, some of my family members would have had me on Skid Row.

But back to the story. Getting off the elevator, I found myself harshly addressed by the receptionist. "Wait over there," she ordered, "it'll be ready in a minute." She obviously thought I was there to pick up and deliver a package.

It was probably what I was wearing that threw her off, faded jeans, an old leather jacket, and running shoes.

If that wasn't enough, she almost flatly refused to believe that I was my nephew's uncle.

"Would you like to see my driver's license?" I asked her. "You'll see we have the same last name..."

When she realized her mistake, she quickly rearranged her face and put on a look reserved only for high officials. She was aglow with friendliness. She was beaming. I could see her aura.

I had seen that look many times before. It was the expression that members of my family wore whenever Reggie deigned to make an appearance.

The receptionist was now bending over backwards

to please me, marveling over the fact that I was the CEO/chairman's uncle. *His* uncle. "Anything I can get you? A soft drink? Coffee? Tea? If I had asked her for an egg roll, she probably would have run out and got one for me.

While waiting, I leafed through some financial magazines, not understanding a word. Finally, a call came through, and the receptionist said, in a low, reverent voice, "you may go in now".

A glass door slid open and there stood a young woman, waiting to escort me down the hall to shrine that was Reggie's office. I entered. He was on the phone.

"Hi," I said. My distracted nephew came around the desk without interrupting his conversation. We did the obligatory hug thing.

Just because I said we don't have anything in common doesn't mean we don't love each other.

Isn't that what certain families are all about? A bunch of people who abuse, take advantage of, ill-treat, torment, reproach, slur, denigrate, curse, stab in the back, slander, bad mouth, denounce, misuse, exploit, vilify, speak ill of, belittle, cheat, and neglect...but love one another?

Getting off the phone momentarily, the CEO/chairman gave me a tour of the offices. Extraordinary architecture. Cathedral-like. On a long table in what seemed like a small chapel with stained-glass windows, stood Reggie's many awards, ornate statuettes of human forms with gigantic wings...massive plaques extolling congratulatory greetings...extravagant creations in Plexiglas and gold...

These were for the fine work Reggie had done in masterminding billion and trillion-dollar deals.

I was impressed. Not only with Reggie, but his

whole set-up. His trappings were sizeable. His own office was fit for someone of the highest imperial order. The views from his windows were stupendous. In the distance, I was sure I could see Italy.

And then they all trooped in. His staff. All Harvard Business School grads. All wearing whiter-than-white Brooks Brothers shirts. All displaying whiter-than-white teeth and exhibiting the same beaming expression as the receptionist.

"This is my Uncle Charlie," Reggie said with a surprising amount of pride and emotion in his voice. He then added, "Author, poet, Clio Award-winning advertising man, screenwriter, songwriter, pianist, artist, traveler, father of three..."

No scrutinizing spotlight could have been more directly trained on a subject than the one on me. This verbal resume of me so impressed the staff—and me for that matter—that I felt I should give an acceptance speech for the Nobel Prize—except that I was speechless. I had never been so neatly (and so exaggeratedly) summed up.

Being somebody is very important to Reggie, and anyone related to him has to be somebody. I can relate to that. I had spent my whole married life trying to make my family into somebodies. But they proved that they were going to be themselves, no matter what.

The CEO/chairman and I then went to lunch as planned. We were chauffeured the two blocks to Reggie's club, no doubt the most exclusive club in the city, all mahogany paneling and crystal chandeliers.

If conversation had been difficult in the past, I didn't have to worry about it on this occasion. Reggie was glued to his cell phone the entire time, barking orders to his underlings regarding a certain merger (in which no mercy was to be shown the other side) and how a multibillion dollar merger was not to exceed one dime (no matter what those sons of bitches demanded). And on and on. It occurred to me that I was dining alone.

But it was okay. Here I was, sitting in regal splendor, albeit in a borrowed jacket and tie provided by the management, dining off the best china, breathing in the same air as some of the richest, most powerful men and women in the world—wasn't that *The Donald* at a table across from us? I was racking this up as a once-in-a-lifetime experience, one I wouldn't have had otherwise.

Best of all, I could take all this in without having to be Reggie. He could be Reggie. That was his job, to be Reggie. Mine was to be me, and I was grateful for that.

At the same time, I knew that anyone observing me, sitting in the hallowed presence of my nephew, Reggie, would be considering me as being a person of distinction, someone to be reckoned with. A real somebody.

And you know something? That's a nice feeling once in a while.

27

Not being able to sit on a park bench near jungle gyms, swings, sandboxes, and swings...if you are a grown man.

So there I was, on a beautiful spring day, and I decided to take my sandwich and newspaper and sit in the park near my office.

Deeply involved in the news of the day, I didn't really notice what was going on around me. The sound of the kids in their section was just as natural as the sounds of the traffic and the birds on the trees.

And then looking up to take in the blue of the sky, I saw them, 27 mothers, or 54 eyes, all staring in my direction.

I immediately read the hostile looks on their faces. They were saying: What are you, a grown man, doing sitting near the kid's playground?

Their blatant expressions of suspicion were understandable given the many horrible cases of child molestation and murder in recent years.

But as the father of three kids of my own, and as someone just as concerned about the dangers kids face, I resent being automatically categorized as a potential sex-offender, just because I'm a man.

Where did that time go, when an adult could say hi to a cute kid and laugh at that kid's antics?

When my son, Michael, was about four years old, he had a friend he called "Man" who lived next door.

Man was a kindly old guy who had grandkids of his own, but was then retired. He liked to work in his garden and smoke his pipe on his veranda and read the newspapers.

Oftentimes, I'd see Michael watching intently as Man might be changing a tire or fixing something in the motor.

Man was Michael's special friend, a grownup, the kind of friend that is extremely vilified in today's world.

When I was a child, I also had a special grownup friend. His name was Charlie and he ran the Chinese laundry in our neighborhood.

The truth is, I wasn't very popular with the kids on my block. One reason can be traced to my individual taste in trading cards. Other boys preferred baseball cards depicting the heroes of the day like Joe DiMaggio and Ted Williams.

I collected Dixie cup lids which, when lifted, revealed the glamorous Technicolor images of Betty Grable and Rita Hayworth.

Because of this "unmanly" pursuit and my abhorrence of any kind of game involving a ball, I was shunned by the other boys. I didn't care. Their idea of fun was horsing around, shooting spitballs at each other, wrestling on the ground.

My idea of fun was exploring the world, being out there on the streets, taking public transport (by the age of six, I was a veteran of the city buses). The only predator to watch out for was the kindly grandmother who would insist on sitting me on her lap if there were no other seats.

New York, in those days, probably wasn't any

safer than it is today for kids, but because there were neighborhoods with people sitting on their porches chatting with neighbors, moms hanging wash on the line, cops on the beat, there was an unofficial neighborhood watch making it harder for kids to be snatched.

It was around this time that I befriended Charlie. He ran the local Chinese laundry and would always insist on buying me an ice cream.

Today, most children are instructed to run in the opposite direction if a man offers to buy them an ice cream. In the '40s and '50s, it wasn't considered anything more than the innocent gesture of an adult who happened to appreciate children.

Charlie's Chinese Laundry was located a few blocks from where I lived in New York City. Charlie, in his meticulously starched white shirt and high collar, was the perfect advertisement for his service. And since my name was Charlie, too, we became immediate friends.

Charlie would see me approaching his storefront with a bunch of my father's shirts tucked under one arm and give me the biggest, most friendly gold-toothed smile you ever saw. Out would come a dime which he would press into my hand. "You buy ice cream," he would say loudly.

Charlie, as I found out, had no family. Nor did he seem to have many friends—except for me. One day, he showed me the badly creased photograph of some Chinese people and uttered one word descriptions of then. Pointing to a woman in the picture, he applied the word "wife." To the children sitting alongside her, he applied the word "children." And then, referring to them all, in a faltering voice, he applied the word "dead."

I have no idea how Charlie's wife and children died or how Charlie came to be in New York. He never told me. But his grief was obvious, even to a child, and it was from my much older, socially adept sister, Irene, that I had a sudden inspiration as how to alleviate this grief.

Entering Charlie's shop one hot day, I parroted Irene's way of issuing an invitation: "If you're not doing anything Saturday night, would you like to come over for dinner?"

Even now, all these many years later, I can still see his face. He was elated. He went happily about his work, washing and ironing shirts with an exaggerated animation, giving me a gold-toothed grin every few minutes.

Of course, it never occurred to me to tell my mother about this. Not that she would have known what to do even if I had told her. To have a Chinese man sitting at the dining room table would have been, for her, as far-fetched as having over the King and Queen of England.

Several evenings later, sitting on the stoop outside our house, I noticed a gentleman in a white suit and hat approaching. As he neared, I saw it was Charlie. I remembered now that I had given him our address, and that he was coming to dinner.

In my knees, a signal began pulsating, a feeling of weakness that was almost painful. It was the first time in my life that I can recall feeling as if the earth was opening beneath me and that I was being swallowed up.

I sat motionless as Charlie walked right up to me, grinned his great grin, and proceeded past me. I was mesmerized by the whiteness of his suit, the knife-edge creases in his trousers, the newly whitened whiteness of his shoes, the perfect shape of his white fedora, the...I snapped out of it and scurried after him to the front door.

Why didn't I bar his way and tell him my mother was sick. Better still, why didn't I tell him she had died and wouldn't be able to serve dinner after all? There were two sets of steps to the front door and on each one of them Charlie would stop, smile, and go on.

Finally, he politely rapped on the door. It took several hundred years for my mother to answer it. We'd always had solicitors in the neighborhood—Fuller Brush men, Hoover salesmen—and she'd always had a prepared speech for them. It was simple and direct. "I'm not interested," she would say, closing the door in their faces before they even had a chance to go into their spiels.

Tonight, she was totally unprepared. A smiling Chinese man stood in the doorway waiting to be invited in.

"I come for dinner," he announced.

My father, a bartender, was gone six nights a week and this was one of them. Had he been there, who knows what might have happened? Knowing my dad, he would have instantly recognized the sweetness of Charlie's nature and would have plied him with corned beef and cabbage as well as great quantities of his bathtub blueberry brandy.

But he wasn't home, and all that welcomed Charlie was the incomprehension on my mother's face.

"You come for what?" she finally uttered.

"I come for dinner," Charlie repeated, his smile even brighter than before.

Mom stood there a moment, still perplexed. And then I heard her say it and I cringed with every word. "You've got the wrong place, mister. I don't have any dinner here," she said, grabbing me inside and closing the door.

I never again visited Charlie's shop. The school

term began shortly after this, and I was rarely sent on errands. Then, months later, during Christmas vacation, my mother sent me out for a few items. Enroute, I bumped into a classmate, Stella Sklar, who was coming from the opposite direction.

Stella and I decided that we would walk backwards while facing the other for as long as we could see the other. I managed, despite all the people on the crowded street, to spot Stella for quite a distance.

And then the sky turned upside down. I don't remember falling backward over the open shop cellar door, nor do I remember being knocked unconscious or being carried up the steps again, but I do remember the sound of a siren in the background growing louder and louder.

I tried to make out the face of one particular man who sat with me the entire time, but because of the concussion, all I could manage was a fuzzy outline.

"You get better," he commanded, worry and distress in his voice. "You get better. I buy you ice cream!"

28

Losing our big city neighborhoods to the corporate world.

The brownstones and tenement buildings that I knew as a child and teenager in Manhattan are now gone. In fact, you would never know they ever existed.

That goes for the mix of interracial families that used to inhabit the buildings along with the grocery shops, butchers, cobblers, restaurants, bars, dry cleaners, news agents, florists, bakeries, shoe shine stands, dress shops, and movie houses that ran lengthwise and across Manhattan.

Even the cop on the beat is a thing of the past. You now call 911 in case of an emergency.

Instead of the tenements and brownstones of old, we have gleaming corporate towers rising thousands of feet upward mingled with luxury condos that only big bonus bank presidents can afford.

When I was going to high school, people actually lived in midtown Manhattan, maybe not in the fancy east side townhouses, but still in midtown. They were everyday people like mechanics, plumbers, factory workers, office workers, barbers and waiters.

Disappearing rapidly today is the first floor walk-up or the railroad flat. True, a lot of those abodes were shabby, even depressing. Still, they were home to countless thousands of people.

To live in midtown today, you have to do it right. You have to be able to tip the doormen at Christmas some exorbitant amount...and not only the day doorman, but the night doorman, janitors, building handymen, and anyone who offers any kind of service in your building.

Meanwhile, the people who used to live in midtown Manhattan have been exiled to regions out of the borough. They are the vast army of commuters who use the rail systems coming out of Connecticut, Westchester, and Long Island. Being squashed like a herring on the New York subways is a way of life.

I once had the supreme privilege of living on East 57th Street. I worked on Lexington Avenue and walked to and from work. This was a perfect situation for me until my wife and I were blessed with the birth of a third child. And so it was time to move because we needed more space. But east side Manhattan rentals had doubled.

The west side of Manhattan in those days was still considered a bargain although those of us who were from the east side would look upon that area with snobbish disdain.

However, in light of the huge increase in east side rentals, my wife and I had no choice but to look westward. We found a large apartment off Riverside Drive and had put down the first month's rent, plus security. We were about to move into the building when we were informed that a murder had taken place there and it would be months before the police would allow new tenants to move in.

With a wife and three kids, what was I to do? We were practically homeless. Correction, we *were* homeless.

Looking through the rentals in the newspaper,

there was a big ad extolling the benefits of living in Lefrak City. It was in Rego Park. And Rego Park was in Queens. Queens! If I had been a snob about moving to the west side of Manhattan, you can imagine how I felt about moving to Queens.

Because there were no Manhattan rentals within my budget, I took the subway out to Rego Park and had a look at the apartment. It was great! It was large, new, and clean. And cheap. About half what it would have cost to move into the West Side place. I took it.

We were happy there. For an hour. But then the Queens vibes started to filter in. Along with the deadliest of people I had ever, in my life, encountered.

For example, riding the elevator with my wife, one day, I spotted the woman from next door who was riding with us. We had never spoken before. I decided to introduce myself and my wife. "Hi," I said, "My name is Charles and this is my wife. You live in 501 and we're in 502 and..."

"Hmmmppppffff," the woman said and without as much as a glance in our direction, turned her back on us. I decided not to introduce us to anyone else in that building.

The woman was the mother of Elliot. This was a kid of around nine or ten years old and a total terror.

One of Elliot's fun things to do was to go from floor to floor and ring for the elevator. As the doors would open, Elliot would not get on, but smile, and as the doors were closing again, give the passengers the finger. Or let go with "FUCK YOU AND DIE!" in a blood-curdling shriek.

He had also set fire to the couch in the entry way, and was in the habit of leaving obscene messages on walls and under people's doors.

On one occasion, he waited at his window as the

window washers descended outside the building. It was then that Elliot opened the window and tried to sever the window washer cords with a kitchen knife.

As truly horrendous was the behavior of Elliot, his mother was even worse.

Day and night you would hear her through our thin walls screaming "ELLIOTTTTTT…"

There was no time limit on her siren-like voice. She could scream "ELLIOTTTTTT" at four in the afternoon or four in the morning.

Having been jolted awake one midnight and not being able to stand it any longer, I opened my door a smidgen as she was screaming for her son in the hall. "Madam," I said, would you kindly…"

"Fuck you and your skinny bitch of a wife," she replied. I quietly closed the door.

And then there were the roaches and rats. This was a fairly new building, but because people left their garbage bags on the floor of the garbage room instead of putting them down the chute, we had a plague of roaches.

With my small children playing on the floors of our apartment, I didn't want them coming in contact with these bugs, or being bitten by something else that might be lurking, like a rat, so I sprayed my apartment, but the roaches still found a way in.

Being that I was an ad agency writer, I then devised a plan. I wrote a number of ads, got them typeset, and placed them in the fifteen garbage rooms of the building.

I can only recall one ad, which read: NOW THAT YOU HAVE LEARNED TO PUT YOUR GARBAGE INTO BAGS, PLEASE PUT THE BAGS DOWN THE CHUTE.

The ads did no good. Nothing did any good. This

place was right out of hell. And so was the neighbor-hood. People walked like the living dead.

My wife was a prisoner five days of the week be-cause there were no ramps for baby carriages out of the building. Requests to the management that they rem-edy this were ignored.

We hated going out unless it was into the car and out to the Hamptons. We especially hated going to the local supermarket because the living dead were either shopping there or working there.

Normally, we would do a big shop on Saturdays since my wife could never get out (and could never find a reliable baby sitter). One late Saturday afternoon, filling our shopping cart with groceries, we were as-tounded to find we couldn't buy the items.

"It's closing time," one of the zombies told us.

"Okay," I said, "we'll just check out our stuff and leave".

"It's closing time," the zombie repeated. "You have to leave now."

And so we had to leave everything behind and find some other place for groceries. One of those small places that charge double for the same item in a super-market.

No doubt there were a lot of nice people and neigh-borhoods in Rego Park, but the people in our building weren't in that group. It was time to get out of Lefrak City and out of Rego Park and out of Queens...but where could we go? It was only May and our lease ran to the following September. We broke the lease, paid the enormous penalty, and called the moving company.

We were going to Vermont. We had a little chalet house in Marlboro which we used in the summers. Be-cause we were literally escaping from this place where we had been so unhappy, we decided to go up earlier than usual.

I would work in the city five days a week, living in a rented room. On Fridays, I would take off for Vermont and spend the weekends. It wasn't ideal, but we had no choice.

As the movers were placing our items in the van, people, including Elliot, were throwing things out their windows. He dropped a Smith-Corona typewriter off their little balcony. "YOU MOTHERFUCKERS, YOU COCKSUCKERS," he screamed" One of the movers sidestepped the typewriter but almost got clobbered by an iron.

"Hey," he said, picking it up, "it's still hot."

It had been raining heavily all the while, but when we were finally in our car and leaving, tolerating a final clunk on the top of the car (a hotplate that slid off the side), the rain started to subside.

As we headed for Vermont, a bright and beautiful rainbow, an omen we decided, formed an arch over the road.

We only briefly lived in Manhattan once more. It was years later. When I could afford it.

29

Designer labels and how people "have to" have them.

There are thousands of people in the world who are obsessed with the designer labels on their clothes. Their identities are tied up with the need to create an image through these labels. Come to think of it, I am one of those people. And the following shows you how complicated and time-consuming the whole thing is. On a number of my caps there'll be the embroidered names of cities, states, and countries I have visited: Los Angeles, Anchorage, Cyprus, Mexico City, Tokyo, Vietnam Dubai, Belgium. On a sweatshirt, there'll be Montana or Hawai'i or Venezuela or South Carolina. On a jacket, Vermont or Australia or Kenya. Aside from business suits, sports jackets and slacks, I own very few clothes that don't broadcast some place I've been to sometime or other during my life. I noticed this the other day when I put on my favorite Windbreaker with the words New York City neatly stitched above the pocket, and was searching for the appropriate cap to go with it. I decided that my Miami cap wouldn't go with it because New York and Miami are both on the east coast, and I wanted a more global feel. My London cap would have been okay, but then I decided I didn't want two cities. My New Zealand cap was out of the question because I didn't feel that two places with "New" in the

name was balanced. I finally settled for my San Diego
cap, but on second thought abandoned that because I
was wearing my San Francisco T-shirt under my New
York Windbreaker, and it just seemed too much to be
wearing two garments from California starting with
"San." I debated as to whether my cap from St. Petersburg was too close due to the "St.," but thought
the heck with it until I realized that people reading my
clothing might not know that I'd bought this particular cap in St. Petersburg, Russia, not St. Petersburg,
Florida although I do happen to have a cap from St.
Petersburg, Florida stuffed somewhere back on my cap
shelf. By the time I was finished dressing, I'd pulled out
just about every sweater, shirt, jacket, and cap I owned,
studying each one, trying to discern the implications of
them being on my body. Were they a good mix? Would
the message they would be relaying be the right one for
my image? After a period of deliberation, I saw plainly
that my clothes were betraying the person I intrinsi-
cally was. What had started out as a simple act of getting dressed so that I could run down to Safeway for a
dozen eggs had turned into a major production. In the
end, I was back to where I had been in the beginning,
confused, lacking in confidence, and annoyed with myself for not having the strength of character and the
conviction of mind necessary to put together an outfit
I could feel good about. I'd tried every combination of
place names before acknowledging that I was doomed
to failure because (sudden revelation) I simply did not
own what I now perceived to be the perfect cap for
the occasion, one from Planet Hollywood in Rio de Ja-
neiro. And so, rather than offend the eyes of onlookers,
I went capless. Like names of places, manufacturers
names also adorn my clothing, The name Gore-Tex is
attached to the hiking boots I have never once gone

hiking in, but which I only wear as a fashion statement. The name Levi Strauss identifies my jeans and Armani is prominently displayed on a number of cotton shirts that are the same exact garments known as long john tops, only 50 times more expensive. The name Cartier sits elegantly on the face of one of my watches while that leader of the watch world, Rolex, vaunts itself on another. Even my eyeglasses tout the name Gucci. And when it comes to underwear, the world will be relieved in the knowledge that I wear Calvin Klein's. But, even though manufacturer's names adorn my clothing, they are not always compatible with what I'm wearing. For example, there is no way that I would wear my John Deere Tractor hat with my Burberry's of London raincoat. And certainly, I would rather go naked than combine my Ralph Lauren pullover with the little alligator (or is it a crocodile?) with a jacket that advertises, in huge type, the initials DKNY. As if all this isn't problematical enough, there's yet another area that adds to the unease, and that's the celebrity garment. Many years ago, I was fortunate enough to see Michael Jackson perform in New York. Can I wear the tie publicizing his name? Or is it passé? That goes for the U2 concert sweatshirt I bought at Wembly. Would either one of them work with the Barrack Obama fanny pack I acquired when he was on the campaign trail in Wisconsin? Or the Three Tenors tank top I couldn't pass up after seeing them at Carnegie Hall? Or the Mickey Mouse earmuffs that I had to have when I visited Disneyland back in '93? These are some of the questions I'm hard-pressed to answer. Others include: When is it permissible to combine hotel logos with those of golf clubs, restaurants, and ski resorts? Or to combine airline logos with those of cruise ship lines that take you down to the Caribbean or with hired helicopters that dangle you above active volcanoes? Does the Jurassic Park dinosaur covering your torso conflict with the 1001 Dalmatians perched on your head? For many of us, clothes with names and images on them is a way of life as I can certainly attest.

But there's one garment where even I draw the line. Monogrammed pajamas.

30

Moving toward one's second childhood while still trying to figure out what happened in the first.

Childhood is that time of life when a person shouldn't have to do much more than be a child. It's comfortable and safe, and therefore, sometimes hard to make the transition to adulthood.

I can attest to that.

In the spring of my high school freshman year, I decided to go to a psychiatrist because I was having the all too common problem of trying to grow up.

Seeing a psychiatrist in the 1950s was an unheard of thing for a 14 year old boy to want to do. Seeking help because you felt you were going crazy was thought to be, ironically, something only a nut would do.

But then, in my family, we did have a history of mental problems. My mom, for example, was convinced that my father was in contact with little green men on the moon who controlled her every thought and action.

Other than for that fact, she was absolutely normal. She ran the house, got my younger brother and me out to school on time, made the meals, made the beds...

It seemed, on the surface, that I was normal, too.

I went to school, had some friends, did my homework, but all this was on the surface.

Puberty was a state of life I had never wanted to enter. I preferred to stay in the far safer regions of childhood. The physical changes I was going through were alarming to me. At the first sign of hair, other than that on my head, I shaved it off with my father's razor. But worse were the mental agonies of self-consciousness and uncertainty.

I kept the fact that I was going to see a psychiatrist secret from my family although I had initially appealed to them, telling them, pleading with them, that I needed professional help. Unfortunately, their ears were clamped shut due to the problems they were having regarding my mother.

I remember driving somewhere with my father and all of a sudden blurting out "I NEED A PSYCHIATRIST NOW!" My father's response, if he had one, was totally unexpressed. It was as if I hadn't said anything at all. For the rest of the journey, he just drove, his eyes focused on the road ahead. That's what it was like going to my father with a problem in those days. Better not talk to the little nutcase, he probably thought.

This is not to say he was a neglectful father. He was a wonderful, loving dad who cared about me and showed it in practical ways. He took an interest in my schoolwork, and he gently corrected me when I was about to do something that would get me in trouble— such as ordering too many records from magazine ads.

He was generous, giving me a good weekly allowance for lunch and carfare to my high school which was located on West 18th Street in Manhattan.

But he never said anything too personal to me such as, "You look depressed, son," or "Have you seen my razor?"

He was a typical father who went to work to make sure his family had a roof over its head. That was his mission in life and probably all he could handle.

I first got the idea of going to a psychiatrist from a school friend, Billy, the only person on earth who seemed to notice how suicidal I looked all the time. He confided in me that he, himself, was manic depressive, whatever that was, and that he had a tendency to want to set fires.

His mother, fearing that her son would become a serial arsonist, had arranged for him to see a Dr. Train on East 54th Street. Billy volunteered that if I wanted, he could get his mother to arrange a session for me with Dr. Train, too.

The price, Billy explained, was $10.00 a visit. That didn't bother me because I could easily save that amount from my allowance.

So I went to see Dr. Train and aside from my manic depressive and fire fiend friend, I only told one other person of the visit.

Later, when the detectives questioned me, it was because I had told this other person. I was in the middle of my history class when a breathless messenger from the principal's office appeared in the doorway. I was to report to the principal immediately.

What was this all about? Were they going to expel me because of the math class I'd cut? I went to the office where I was confronted by two looming men in fedoras. These were the detectives. They wanted to know about Dr. Train.

The person I had confided in, someone I had sworn to secrecy, someone who vowed never to breathe a word, was a girl named Mikki who went to my school. She was from Los Angeles and, according to her, had lived a wild Hollywood life before being forced to move to New York when her father, who she said she hated, had been relocated there.

Mikki and I started hanging out together, and made an incongruous pair, a gangly guy and a stunning Hollywood brunette, each of us only 14 years old.

We liked to spend time in Greenwich Village, not far from our high school in Chelsea. There, we would pretend that we were as beat as the coolest beatniks who were a common sight.

Mikki and I would goad each other to do outrageous things, to see who could top who. I might dare her to steal a tablecloth from a café and she would then, circumspectly, remove it and tuck it into her jacket as we ate. Then we would complain bitterly to the waitress that all the other tables had tablecloths and ours didn't—at which point, the waitress would spread another tablecloth out for us. And then it would be my turn to steal the tablecloth.

On other occasions, we might come up with a joint idea. Like the time we decided to stage an impromptu MGM musical on Waverly Place. She was Cyd Charrise and I was Gene Kelly as we sang and clashed trash can covers together, swung around light poles, danced up and down brownstone steps, and ended the number with me poised on the hood of a Yellow Cab that had stopped at a red light—the driver too astounded to yell.

We both loved riding the subway and staring at people. Our goal was to outstare certain people we picked at random. Mikki always did the picking and she always chose stern looking men who, she said, reminded her of the father she loathed. We would briefly strategize that these men were tyrants who beat their children and deserved the most contemptuous of our stares.

For me, it was just a game, but perhaps it was this need to needle stern-looking men that led Mikki to needle the one stern-looking male in my family, my Uncle Ike. He was my mother's youngest brother, a no-nonsense, ex-Marine drill instructor who had fought at Guadalcanal and Iwo Jima during WWII. Now a bachelor of 35, he was a cop.

Late one evening, wandering along Riverside Drive, far from our usual territory, we found ourselves in front of my uncle's apartment building. Why not ring the bell and see if he was off-duty, we thought? He was, as it turned out, at home having a beer, and in we trooped, two sophisticates, out on the town.

Mikki, who could have passed for a woman in her 20s, asked for a glass of wine and got a ginger ale. Between sips, she started to grill my uncle, asking all sorts of personal questions. What was his salary? Did he have a girlfriend? Was he a homosexual?

Ike, known in the family for his controlling manner, tried to take back the power and what followed was a struggle between him and Mikki to get the upper hand. It was evident that Uncle Ike had become, for Mikki, the forceful male figure that she was in the habit of challenging.

The fierce battle of the wills, played out in words, went on until my uncle said that he would ask the questions from that point on. Did her parents know she was out at night? Did they know she wore a lot of makeup? Did they know she drank wine when she could get it?

It was then that Mikki, holding the trump card, asked, "Did you know that your nephew is seeing a psychiatrist by the name of Dr. Train?"

That statement, which would seem totally harmless today, was viewed differently all those years ago when people were so shrinkophobic.

I don't recall, in my memory's eye, seeing much of a reaction in my uncle other than an imperceptible start. Looking at Mikki, I could see that the victory was hers.

Her intuition told her that this rough, gruff, somewhat uptight man would feel stigmatized being the uncle of a mentally unbalanced person. She had stared him down, but more than that, she had worded him down.

We left his apartment shortly afterwards, she gaily saying goodbye and he hardly nodding.

Of course, Mikki's betrayal in telling my uncle about my visit to a psychiatrist ended our friendship. Nothing was said. It was just over. The other thing was that even though I hadn't fully figured it out, I was aware of the adult chemistry which had happened between Mikki and my uncle, and I felt jealous and inadequate, like the skinny, awkward, innocent teenager that I was.

And now I was being questioned by these two detectives who wanted to know about Dr. Train.

"Did he touch you?" the toughest of the two detectives asked me. I had no idea what he was talking about.

"We shook hands," I replied, thinking that perhaps this was what he meant. When this didn't seem to please him, I volunteered how Dr. Train had held up one colored pencil after another asking what each color meant to me. That was it. For 50 minutes. The colored pencils routine had cost me 10 bucks and I hadn't felt any better leaving Dr. Train's office than I felt arriving.

I was confused as to how this "investigation" got started in the first place—and then I realized that when Mikki ratted on me to my uncle, he must have called the detectives. After all, he was a cop, and those guys were his buddies.

Psychiatrists at that time were put in the same category as weirdoes, commies, and felons. And people who went to them weren't that far behind. The detectives warned me about associating with Dr. Train, and then left.

Being an impressionable teen, I decided that I wouldn't be attending any more sessions with psychiatrists—not that I would have returned to Dr. Train and his collection of colored pencils, anyway.

My uncle, before his death from cancer, eleven years later, at age 46, never mentioned the incident to me, nor did I to him.

But I knew he had to have been the person who called the detectives. As for Mikki, she dropped out of high school several months later and went off with a man who was much older than she was. I think he was 19 years old.

Mikki was, or so it seemed, mentally and physically far beyond any of her schoolmates. After her departure, I missed her greatly, even though we never again spoke to one another after the visit to see my uncle. But for the short time that I did know her, I was able to get away from being the gawky ectomorph and was able to enjoy a freedom I didn't feel otherwise.

I often wonder whatever happened to Mikki. Did she return to Hollywood? Did she ever reconcile her problems with her father? Did she go into show business? She was a beautiful girl who could have easily made it as a model.

Actually, and I'm not sure of this, but there was a time when I was in the Marines, that I thought I recognized her in a sleazy calendar shot. The nude girl in the photo could have been Mikki, a startlingly older, extremely hardened Mikki, with peroxide hair and an expression that said she'd seen it all. Maybe it was her. I like to think it wasn't.

Years later, when no one thought anything about going to a psychiatrist and when my career and my marriage came to a halt, I picked up where I left off with Dr. Train.

My new doctor and I discussed many things, but I never thought to tell him of how I would ride the subway as I once did with Mikki—although never staring at people at we once did—but just to take a journey back in time, when the world was fresh, and life lay ahead for a young boy and a young girl.

31

Making boys play sports when they don't want to play sports.

I know very little about baseball or football. And I'm not interested in learning more. As a child, I just saw these two national obsessions as silly games in which people hit a ball or threw one around.

And I still see it that way. It really annoys me when the TV program, Jeopardy, is replaced by Saturday night football.

But back in the days when I was growing up, boys were expected to excel in sports, or at least play them as best possible. If they didn't, the common perception was that there had to be something wrong with them, even something unnatural.

It was thought that the non-participant was almost un-American. And there was a certain resentment toward him because he didn't seem able to be a proper team member or to lose his individuality.

Sports were "the manly pastime", complete with broken bones and concussions. Any young boy not partaking was automatically categorized as less than a man. A coward, effeminate, someone who belonged in the homemaking classes with the girls.

My steadfast refusal to get involved got me into a lot of scrapes, but before I continue, a little background; and a bit of New York history.

In the first 20 years after WWll, there was a migration of people from the crowded streets of Manhattan, Brooklyn, and the Bronx to the open spaces of Long Island. In the dozens of brand new neighborhoods that sprung up, there were such novelties as trees and meadows and lakes and streams. And ball parks.

I became a temporary resident of Nassau County, Long Island at the age of ten. My mother, who'd been putting off a nervous breakdown ever since I'd known her, finally decided to have one. And while she was shipped off to the Creedmore Institution for the Insane for a year, my younger brother, Jackie, and I were shunted off to live with an older sister, Irene, and her husband, Arnie, and their year-old son, Richard, in a town called Elmont.

Former farmlands, the terrain of this area was transformed into neat plots of land upon which little houses were built. This was where returning soldiers, sailors, and Marines of WWll could raise their families.

Those people may have loved it, but for me, the transition was not an easy one. I was a New York City person, not a Nassau County person. I dwelled in the skyscraper world of concrete and steel, not in the unpolluted air or on the open playing fields of Elmont, Nassau County, Long Island.

This marked difference in cultures made me uncomfortable at first. Where were the cramped classrooms with the desks dating back to the beginning of the century? Where were the neurotic, older teachers such as Mrs. Latte whom each day had a different student brush her hair?

Some things I did approve of. For example, I was no longer expected to wear a jacket, shirt and tie, but could actually wear jeans and a sports shirt. Even sneakers.

The school I went to, Alden Terrace, was brand new, with round, free-standing tables and chairs that were of blond wood. I had never seen blond wood before. The teachers were young and vibrant. Miss Lawrence and Mr. Linden were both only 25 years old.

Miss Lawrence was tall and beautiful with dark short hair parted on the side. She was gentle and helpful rather than crabby and sarcastic as were the teachers I was used to in the city.

Mr. Linden was enthusiastic and fair. He had been in the Army Air Corps from 1943 to 1945 and had two suits. On one day, he would wear a complete suit. The next day he would wear the jacket from one suit and the trousers from the other, an order to be reversed the following day. And then he would wear the second suit in its entirety.

The mere fact that I noticed how people dressed showed an interest in fashion that was almost subversive in a young boy.

Equally subversive were my weekend activities, viewed as distinctly strange by the other kids. After all, what kind of person wanted to spend all his Saturdays at the public library devouring back issues of National Geographic Magazine instead of taking part in healthy sports?

The answer was a skinny, near-sighted, book-loving, introverted product of a dark, treeless, concrete, urban environment. In other words, me.

Maybe it was because I had such bad vision—something that wasn't discovered until I was 10 years old—that led to a disinterest in sports. Not being able to see a ball properly, made it impossible to hit one or catch one. Before my eye exam, I never thought to complain because I just naturally assumed that this was the way all people saw things. Blurry.

And after I did find out, I was damned if I would wear the glasses issued to me, especially after the fool of an eye doctor informed me that I would now be called four-eyes. This was an appellation that carried extreme penalties meted out by the school toughs, of which there were many. Besides, I preferred a blurry, anonymous existence to a sharp, clear one.

In later years, I came to believe that some children with poor vision don't want to see what's going on around them. I certainly didn't. There was so much disharmony in my family that I came away from it with one other psychological affliction besides the poor eyesight, rounded shoulders which, from what I understand, is the posture of someone attempting to protect his or her heart.

So half-blind, and hunched over like an old man, I lurched to school each day, friendless except for one boy. This was Walter, who didn't challenge me just because I wasn't doing "childhood" in the prescribed manner.

Walter informed me one day in the cafeteria that the other kids didn't seem to like me but that he didn't care about any of that and that he didn't mind being friends with me.

He was that rare breed of humanitarian who never had to prove himself to attain respect from others. Walter certainly had my respect, and when he defied all convention to befriend me, I felt both honored and appreciative.

He would tell the other kids, with impunity, to leave me alone when they were looking for a victim to harass. They would instantly back off, even though they couldn't understand how he could pal around with the likes of me.

But, great friend that he was, there was one person

Walter couldn't tell to leave me alone.

That was Coach Burns who decided that I would play baseball, whether I wanted to or not. It didn't matter to him that I had absolutely no throwing arm or that I couldn't see the ball coming toward me when I was at bat, much less hit it.

Coach Burns liked to think of himself as democratic. When playing against other teams from other schools, he let the kids choose the players and the positions. In this instance, I was, understandably, left unassigned.

Standing there, the lone kid, with all the other kids secure as team members, I felt the true weight of rejection. Having to do something with me, Coach Burns finally relegated me to the right field. This was where I was to be stationed, game after game, where nary a ball ever went.

It was on a interminable sticky, hot June afternoon that I stood, as usual, unblessed, unloved, and alone on that field. Even the sun glared down unrelentingly on me. Putting my glove hand, palm outward, to protect my burnt, near-sighted eyes from the glare, I felt a sudden jolt on my shoulder that reverberated throughout my entire body. The ball, by some miracle, had found me. It had actually hit me and was lying on the ground near my feet. Like a drowning man reaching for a life preserver, I tried to grasp it.

I heard my team yelling for me to pick up the ball and throw it, and I'd like to say that it stayed in my hand when I picked it up, but it didn't. It fell, and I picked it up again; this time it stayed in my palm until the moment I finally got it airborne.

Piecing it all together, this was the scenario: I was in the right field. Apparently I came into contact with the ball (or vice versa) at the end of the game (bottom of the ninth, as it is called.) We were up by one point, there was one out, and the opposing team had a man on first and a man on second.

I, on my second attempt, snatched the ball off the ground and directed it toward Richie DeMarco, a kid who came racing toward me yelling something I couldn't make out. It was he who relayed the ball to second base thereby causing the third out.

We won the game and more than that, it was the final in a series of games in our school district, and we were announced the season champs. It was a major victory. People were screaming and jumping up and down.

How I got on the shoulders of the other players on my team, I don't know—there I was, perched high and displayed around the field like a trophy. And although I was never again to catch a ball or hit one, I was a legend for at least a week.

So this story has a happy ending, and while it didn't completely cancel out all the pain I suffered the previous years, or prevent my exclusion in sports in later years, it did cancel out a lot of it.

When they talk of "angels in the outfield" I know I definitely had mine. The only thing is, why did I have to go through all that nonsense, and what did it prove?

If kids don't feel like being jocks, it's their choice, not society's.

32

Municipally sponsored fireworks: A huge waste of taxpayer's money

Okay, so I'm a spoilsport. I'm the one who begrudges anyone having fun with fireworks, like all those kiddies, all those adults, and all those teens setting off the leftover 4th of July fireworks on July 5th and July 6th.

If it seems un-American of me being the person who stands there looking grim while everyone is as "lit up" as the fireworks themselves, it's because I'm the one who would like to see fireworks permanently banned from our skies.

I dislike fireworks, all that the sizzling, banging, hissing, screaming display. To heck with the rockets bursting in air. It gives me a headache.

But it's more than that. I don't enjoy seeing public money being used to put on this yearly cracker orgy. Nor do I enjoy reading about the eyes, hearing, limbs and lives lost to pyrotechnics. Or whole forests being set aflame. Or dogs and cats hiding under beds.

Ever witness how people act once the sun goes down on July 4th? It's quite a picture. Kids go crazy. If they were never hyper before, they certainly are now. It's like they're on invisible pogo sticks, or speed, or both.

Adults, meanwhile, go around wearing these truly insane facial expressions. They seem to be experiencing something similar in an orgasm. There's the rush, the excitement, the climax...the letdown.

The only other adrenalin charge that's similar is the one usually reserved for the maniacal ripping open of carefully wrapped Christmas presents. Again, the rush, the excitement, the climax...the letdown (oh no, not another tie from Aunt Edith!)

All this for a series of flowers gone berserk in the sky.

It was last July 4th and I was walking past a bunch of people setting off a massive fireworks display in the street. Everyone was in the usual frenzy of anticipation. I noticed one young child, a boy of about five, whose head was in direct line of the missiles just about to be deployed.

In another moment, the kid's head would have gone into orbit, had I not yelled for him to get out of the way.

The possibility of a headless child did nothing to dispel the glazed-eyed onlookers. Someone in the crowd actually said, "Hey, buddy, what's your problem?"

"Oh nothing," I said, "I just thought a decapitation might dampen the festivities...must have been wrong."

Long before I'd even finished the sentence, they'd lost interest. Preferring, instead, to jerk their heads upward hungrily awaiting the next burst of sparkles, noise...polluted air.

Then there was the time I was driving along when I noticed someone's roof was on fire. It wasn't as if the house was deserted or anything. I saw people out front, women with babies in their arms, men with explosives in theirs.

I didn't want to be a buttinsky, but I felt I should roll down the car window and mention the blaze that no one else seemed to notice.

"Uh," I said, "maybe you should turn around and look at the house over there? The one going up in flames?"

Gazing over their shoulders, they seemed to deliberate: Should we watch the rest of the show? Or let the house burn down?

These people I'm describing are the same people who line up at the fireworks sales kiosks every June. They may not pay their credit card debt, but don't seem to mind spending their cash on mineshells, missiles, and rockets.

Well, it's their money, and they can watch it go up in smoke if they wish. My protest, again, has to do with public money.

When a village, town, or city puts on a huge fireworks display, it is spending our tax money.

And every village, town, and city loses money, and lots of it. And yet, this so-called patriotic tradition continues.

What would be even more patriotic would be to use the money on the things that would improve life.

Just think how much money we could collect if every village, town, and city in America were to cease providing fireworks in favor of doing the following:

Hiring more teachers for our schools.

Raising teacher's salaries.

Re-instating such discontinued school programs as music instruction and physical training.

Improving school lunches.

Purchasing new books for schools and libraries.

Creating homeless shelters.

Creating retraining programs for people out of work.

Retrofitting buildings and bridges.

Supporting the arts.

Repairing roads and highways.

Creating free medical clinics.

Creating additional aid to the handicapped.

Creating programs for kids who find it hard to learn.

Creating scholarships for brilliant students.

Creating drug awareness programs.

...These are just some of the areas the money saved on banning fireworks could improve.

One often hears of a town or community canceling something or other due to cost constraints, but rarely is there a cancellation in fireworks displays. Those seem sacred, untouchable; here to stay.

City officials regularly vote to keep this "time-honored tradition" in place. "My kids would kill me if I voted to stop the display," said one such official recently.

Ironically, the statistics show that 90% of those killed or maimed are kids and young people up to the age of twenty. And this guy is worried his kids would have a hissy fit?

Everything about the 4th of July seems unhealthy, from the greasy frankfurters and hamburgers to the cholesterol-laden potato salad to all the alcohol that's drunk during this extremely stupid and dangerous ritual.

It's more pathetic than patriotic.

Think about it.

33

Safe, sunny destinations that are anything but...

Let's take Hawai'i. It was another day in paradise and I had decided to get out for a walk on Waikiki Beach and to enjoy the cloud-shrouded view of Diamond Head in the distance.

The beach itself was empty of people, but then, as I walked a bit further I noticed two girls in bikinis sprawled out on their blankets fully intent upon getting a suntan.

I surmised that they were from the mainland and that this was probably their two week vacation. It looked like they were determined to enjoy every minute of it no matter what.

One of the girls sat up and applied some suntan lotion to the supine girl next to her. And then she lay back down.

This was a typical scene on the beach except for one thing. It was raining.

It was obvious that those girls, like so many other tourists, hadn't been given much weather information while still at home, nor did they seek it.

The policy in the islands is to keep certain things about vacationing there hush-hush for fear people will stay away. And the weather is one of them.

"Sure, it rains," a travel agent will tell you. "On

and off, like any other tropical location, but you get plenty of sun, even in December."

Chances are that travel agent has never been to Hawai'i in December because it can rain continuously for days on end... in November, January, and February, too.

Not only that, but it can be suffocatingly humid. But the tourist board doesn't want you to know that, either.

There's also something else the tourist board doesn't want you to know—that methamphetamines are rampant in the islands and so is crime.

Crime in paradise is nothing new. I know, because I once lived in Waikiki, many years ago.

I lived on the Ala Wai Canal which divides Honolulu and Waikiki. Every so often, the mugged and murdered bodies of elderly tourists were found floating in the canal.

All this was kept secret from the mainland for many years, but was, finally, in the early 90s, reported.

The population of Hawai'i has more than tripled in the past 50 years and so has the level of murder, rape, aggravated assault, burglary, and theft.

For myself, I experienced criminal intent several times. The first time was when my wife and I parked and locked our rental car on a bluff overlooking the home of Doris Duke.

We were only out of the car a few minutes, but during that time, someone had cut into the door with a sharp instrument. Had we been gone another minute, the thief would have been able to open that door and take off with my wife's handbag.

Stopping at a Waikiki police station to report the attempted crime, we showed an officer the gash in the car.

"Happens all the time," was all he said in that happy "Island Boy" manner Hawaiians have. "Not even worth filing a report."

And when we returned the car to Avis, the response was the same.

"No probbbblem," the agent said. "Don't worry about it. And make sure you come back to Hawai'i soon, hear?"

This kind of casual attitude gives the impression that the people in Hawai'i are brainwashed by the Chamber of Commerce to never reveal any of the lesser attractive aspects of this fabled playland.

The whole idea, it seems, is to keep intact that vision of swaying palms, balmy breezes, and hula dancers for which Hawai'i is known, a vision that has been drilled onto the imaginations of mainlanders and other unsuspecting people.

But what is really lurking under those swaying palms? And what is going on in the heads of the city planners? Coming to Waikiki, people most certainly want to see the magnificent views of Diamond Head, but those views are getting harder and harder to come by. The construction of 40 story skyscrapers has taken over Waikiki. The streets of that district are almost as dark as the cavernous concrete canyons of Chicago and New York.

To glimpse Diamond Head without the buildings, you have to either be on the water, or at the lagoon near the Hilton Hawaiian Village. There, the Waikiki of old can then be conjured up, but move your eyes a little to the left and the illusion is destroyed by the endless lineup of hotels..

My wife and I used to rent a condo on the other side of O'ahu in Makaha which was heavily guarded against criminal activity. Still, it wasn't completely fortified to keep crime out.

One night as my wife and I were sleeping, I dreamed someone had come into our apartment. I was then awakened by a noise in the entry way. It actually *was* someone coming into the apartment!

There he was, a menacing presence in our living room. Suddenly, my adrenalin went to work and I was about to rush him, even throw him over the balcony. This is not to say I'm powerfully built or that he would have flown off the balcony very gracefully.

But at that moment, there was a loud knock on the door. It was security. They'd seen the intruder on their close circuit cameras as he was riding the elevator, and in checking, found that he had been the previous tenant of this unit, rather than the current one. The security people got him out of there.

According to the front desk clerk next morning, he had checked out but had reported losing his key. Since this was not an establishment that changed keys with each new guest, he was able to get into our apartment.

Later that day, I was hiking the three miles from Makaha to Kaena Point when I saw a car as it whizzed past me at a speed that whipped up a breeze on this otherwise breezeless day. As the driver passed, I saw he was wearing a huge grin. Shortly after, a police car came chasing after him. The driver of the chased car was obviously enjoying himself.

On another occasion, I was driving along when I saw a huge yellow shape in my rear view mirror. It was bearing down on me, so I pulled over and let it pass. It was a school bus filled with kids. The driver was speeding.

And then I saw the police were chasing him, too.

When I got back to my condo, I was curious as to what had happened to the bus driver. The police operator refused to acknowledge that there had been an incident with a bus or a bus driver.

I insisted there had been.

The operator insisted there hadn't.

And then I got it.

This was Hawai'i, land of silence, where things happen that are never reported.

Hawai'i isn't unique in this respect. Anywhere a natural disaster, such as an earthquake, takes place, there's a tendency to cover up the extent of damage or the number of fatalities.

It was reported after the 1906 San Francisco earthquake and fire that there were 250 fatalities. Many years later, mass graves in the Presidio revealed thousands more.

After the Northridge/Los Angeles earthquake of 1994, I was stopped by security police when I was taking a photo of the damage in a local shopping mall. Very little true reporting came out of that disaster. For example, street after street in San Fernando was razed to the ground. The area was devastated.

Denial is the name of the game. Tourism is big business. Big business is also big business. If a company is planning to relocate to a certain area, bringing with it jobs and revenue, it's thought by city councils to keep bad news from reaching certain ears.

So this is why it's to your benefit to learn not just about your vacation destination and what goes on there, but anywhere you're about to relocate...before you get on a plane.

34

People you would never in a million years associate with...if you didn't have to work with them.

I once had a friend named Ray Sherman. I considered him as I would a brother. He lived in Paris and was the creative director of an advertising agency.

I lived in London where I was a copy group head at the Collett Dickenson Pearce Advertising Agency. Ray and I met when he was an art director at this same agency. He was from New York, I was from New York. We became fast friends. Our wives became fast friends.

When he took the creative director job in Paris, we continued our four-way friendship, visiting each other many times either in England or France.

One of Ray's ideas was to interest a leading London advertising agency in opening a branch office in Paris with himself as the head. He did all the unpaid legwork and all the research, laboring long into the night. He flew back and forth across the channel, putting together all the pieces.

The London people were impressed. After three years of negotiations, they told Ray it was a "go." Ray was ecstatic. He finally had the agreement that he'd worked so hard to get.

All that was left was to sign contracts. It was arranged that Ray, and the team of people he'd chosen to work with him, would fly to London where pen would be put to paper.

On the way to Charles De Gaulle airport in a taxi, Ray was beaming. This was, for him, the deal of a lifetime. He had worked very hard for this and now it was about to happen. It was then, by Ray's account, that one of the people he'd recruited informed him of a change in plans.

"What do you mean a change of plans?" Ray asked. Why would somebody he'd recruited be telling him of a change of plans? This was his baby. If anyone would know of a change of plans, it would be him.

"Ray," the man said, "You're out."

Ray regarded the man a moment. He had no idea what he was talking about.

"What I'm telling you, Ray, is that you are no longer part of the equation. Here, read this."

Ray, euphoric just a moment earlier, now came back down to earth. Still looking at the man, he took a letter written on the London agency's letterhead and learned that he was, as the man said, out.

By Ray's account, the letter said something about him not being someone they felt could handle the new agency. Wait, he thought, there was something surreal about this whole thing. What were they saying? That he couldn't handle the very brainchild he'd created—this idea that he'd fed and nurtured along and had brought to life?

The London agency would, in time, open an office in Paris without Ray, using everything he had supplied—the business plan, the research, the marketing plan. It would, in less than a year, become a major force, while Ray, due to the shock, would become something akin to a vegetable.

When this happened, I was also in shock as Ray was one of my best friends. I persuaded him to spend some time with my wife and me in London. Each day, I would walk him around Richmond Park, a vast expanse near my home in West London. Arm in arm we would walk, with me as the nursing attendant, and Ray the hunched over, weeping patient.

Betrayal is common in the business world. I've suffered it myself many times. And by people I trusted. One such person was Blaston McCoy, a director of television commercials. I'd been introduced to him years before by John Nicolls who was the creative director of Royds Advertising, London.

John had a network of associates, one of them being Blaston. In fact, it appears that there was a group of extremely successful British businessmen who were members of what might be described as a secret society. I, myself, had I not been a wild American, might have been inducted into this society.

Being an American, wild or not, was tough in London in those years. People were fond of reciting the ancient wartime slogan about Americans being "overpaid, oversexed, and over here…"

To which I would inevitably reply that the British were underpaid, undersexed and under Eisenhower!"

Comments like that didn't exactly endear me to people in a country not my own, but John Nicolls never pulled that "American" putdown stuff on me. He never used the term, "This is Charles, our American," in the way that other British people did. As if everyone had an American of their own.

John and I were respectful of each other, and although I was never given a key to his club, he always let it be known we were friends. Through his contacts, he kept me in work for years, writing and making radio and television commercials as well as creating print campaigns.

There was usually an element of humor in all of this work. One campaign for Deinhard Green Label Wine read: "The soufflé sank, the duck was dry, and the peas were like bullets. It could have been a disaster." The premise being that the wine saved the evening.

A second ad read: "The meeting ran late, I couldn't find a taxi, and computer-dating fixed me up with my ex-wife. It could have been a disaster. Same premise.

The first of the TV spots I did for John was for Airwick Solid, the room deodorizer. In it, a zookeeper showed how the odors made by Maisie, the resident elephant, were dispelled. "Before Airwick Solid, I had to hold my nose when walking into Maisie's quarters, but now I don't mind going in there. And you know something? Neither does Maisie!"

This, and other spots I wrote and produced earned us a number of awards, and this is where Blaston McCoy came in. John asked me if we could try him out as the director on some of our commercials, and I agreed. Blaston was not the most talented director in London, but he was capable and easy to work with.

I not only used him for productions I was doing with John, but for the round of TV spots I wrote and produced independently of John. One such assignment was for the Bank of Scotland.

I had worked quite a bit in Edinburgh, and my Bank of Scotland contact there had one stipulation: If I was going to get this assignment, the director I chose would have to be extremely good with clients. Blaston McCoy fit the bill perfectly.

And so it came to pass that the production went extremely well. Blaston was extremely diplomatic.

He even invited the clients to look at a scene set-up through the viewfinder, something few other directors would think of doing. It was a wrap without even the slightest incident, thanks to Blaston.

My involvement was finished at that point. Post-production was entrusted to Blaston who had his own production company. I took off to do another assignment, but would check in regularly with Blaston to see if there was anything I could help him with.

And then, something rather strange happened. Blaston McCoy disappeared.

His production company in London was suddenly vacated. What had happened? There was no word of where he'd gone. I tracked down Jonathan, his assistant, who claimed he didn't know anything more than I did.

I spoke to John Nicolls who was also in the dark. It was a big mystery, one that became clear a few months later. While having lunch with the Edinburgh people who'd hired me for the Bank of Scotland spots, they told me what had happened.

Apparently, Blaston had embezzled the funds entrusted to him for Technicolor processing. The amount was 30,000 pounds sterling. Shortly after the commercials were made, the bank was notified by Technicolor that the money had never been paid them. Terrified of scandal, the bank hadn't taken legal action, nor were they planning to.

I was amazed and grateful that the people in Edinburgh hadn't suspected me as being part of this theft since I was the one who'd brought Blaston in. But they never did, as proved by the fact that we worked together a number of times after.

About a year later, I was in New York freelancing, and walking down the hall of a Madison Avenue ad

agency, I bumped smack into Blaston McCoy. Where-
upon I not only knocked him against a wall, but cursed
him out for stealing the money.

"Hold it, hold it," Blaston had said. "What are you
talking about? I didn't steal any money. I'd been planning to shut down my operation in London for years,
and finally did. If you like, I'll fly back to Scotland with
you and meet with these guys."

Sucker that I am, I believed Blaston. And for the
next few years, whenever I worked in New York, Blaston and I would get together. I even hired him on commercial shoots. As usual, he was always highly competent, if not top rank.

And then it happened again, the disappearance.
And I surmised that he'd ripped off some production
fund (luckily not mine, this time), and kicked myself
for believing him regarding the Edinburgh heist.

Meanwhile, my friend, John Nicolls, became ter-
minally ill with bone cancer. I spent a couple of weeks
with him when he was in his last stages of the disease.
When he entered the hospice in Salisbury, we were like
two mischievous kids, sneaking out for wheelchair ex-
cursions on the grounds.

There he would be, dressed in a hospital gown and
with his hair flying as we would careen down the paths,
laughing all the way.

Eventually, the nurses restricted us to the parking
lot, and even there, we had fun discussing the different
cars, the Jags, the Roll Royces, and the Mercedes.

One day, while we were discussing the past, I asked
him: "Did Blaston McCoy take that money?"

John looked at me and thought for a moment.
Then he said, "Yes, he did."

I've always been grateful to John for so many
things, and especially that confession. He had known

Blaston very well, and had not wanted to squeal on him, but all these years later, he let me know that he was aware of this theft. A week later, he was dead.

As for Ray Sherman, the man I started this story with, he and his wife abandoned our friendship in favor of remaining friends with my ex-wife.

Not only that, but he badmouthed me every chance he got. Why he felt compelled to do this, I will never know.

There was closure regarding Blaston McCoy thanks to John, but I still feel pain when I think of Ray, and how he so brutally let go of our friendship.

35

Trying to open a vacuum-sealed plastic product pack.

I get the medicine home, pills in those kind of push through packets. Only try as I might, they won't push through. So I take a pair of scissors and cut around each pill. No luck. They are hermetically sealed in plastic. Final resort, teeth. When they don't work, down the hatch the pill goes, plastic and all. My hope is that when this little plastic packet comes into contact with my stomach acid, that will do the job.

Everyday, people struggle to open vacuum sealed packaging, and many times, they don't succeed. Not long ago, I read a newspaper account about an elderly man who lived in a remote area, and who kept to himself. A neighbor who lived 20 miles away would bring in the provisions for the old guy and then not see him for a month or so.

When found dead, he was said to have been suffering from severe malnutrition. But it wasn't as if he was out of food. Ironically, there was plenty of it in his refrigerator and pantry.

Instead of canned and frozen foods, the usual fare, the neighbor thought a change of diet would be welcomed, and so he brought in vacuum sealed turkey, vacuum packed ham, and vacuum packed chicken. There was mixed lettuce in those plastic containers with a plastic binding.

None of these had been opened and like this elderly gent, many of these items had long ago expired.

Vacuum packing, in this case, turned out to be a murder weapon, because for someone who was old, with arthritic hands, there was no way in hell to get those packs open.

It's understandable how food products have to be protected from the crazies out there whose usual way of getting back at the human race is to mix broken glass in with Halloween candy or to add something lethal to a jar of applesauce.

This is the age of consumer paranoia…and maybe with good reason, seeing as there was a woman some years back who took what she thought was a Tylenol and wound up taking cyanide.

And because since 9/11, the public is apt to find any excuse to panic, whether justified or not.

But this whole vacuum packed thing is going too far. It doesn't just have to do with food, but with non-edible products, like combs, batteries, toiletries, and you name it.

What are these manufacturers thinking? That we're all Arnold Schwartzeneggers who can rip all that plastic apart without even trying?

Vacuum packing should safeguard things that go in the mouth (or some other orifice). Those should be packed in plastic, but with some instruction as to how to release the contents. Instructions, by the way, with nearsighted grannies in mind.

When it comes to things that don't go in the mouth (or some other orifice) what exactly is all the protection for?

There's also a danger associated with the heavy plastic that's being used. Cut it with scissors (often the only way to get it open) and those sharp edges are like knives. One slip of the wrist, and you've had it

And what about jars and containers not vacuum packed but still hard to open? I was just thinking that if my grandmother was alive today, she would be plumb out of luck trying to open even a jar of peanut butter. It's as if those jars are closed with industrial wrenches.

What we need is a team of strongmen right in the store. They would be out-of-work body builders welcoming some form of employment that utilizes those awesome, but otherwise useless, muscles.

They would be on hand to open packaging, or jars and, of course, vacuum sealed plastic wrapped items as soon as we made the purchase so we wouldn't have to wrestle with same.

The problem is, no self-respecting man would be seen dead going to another man to open a package.

There are exceptions. Yours truly, for example. Though I'm an ex-Marine, I would welcome the opportunity to have some of that vacuum-packed stuff opened for me.

The truth is, I'm just about the wimpiest ex-Marine I have ever known. To fix something or assemble something, I'm hopeless. Recently a friend of mine, Mark Prusinowski, was over at my house.

I had him assemble a vacuum cleaner, fix the front doorbell, and to see if he could figure out why the garbage disposal unit was not working.

As I told him, "It's so nice to have a man around the house." Too bad he doesn't visit that often.

Meanwhile, I have to grapple with opening everything. To make it easier, I recently ordered, through a catalog, a razor sharp pocket knife to cut through heavy plastic packaging.

Only to discover, when it arrived, that it was encased in the stuff.

36

Playing the corporate game:
Covering for the boss.

An unwritten aspect to any job, when working for someone else, is to protect that person from embarrassment and humiliation.

Taking the blame for the boss' often asinine mistakes is common; not being acknowledged is even more common.

Regardless of acknowledgement, you get the feeling that some underlings would shield the boss from danger with their very lives.

In truth, there is nothing altruistic about this. By protecting the boss, they are obviously protecting their jobs, the true motivation behind their actions.

One of the reasons I didn't always get along when working for a company was because I never played the game. That was evident when my boss, a famous ad agency creative director, told me, "Charlie, you are a one of the best writers we've got, you've created outstanding campaigns, you're great with clients...and there is no place for you in this agency."

I knew the reason for my dismissal was my apolitical attitude, my refusal to assist the powers that be in terms of their ego quests or to suck up to them.

It wasn't that I felt superior to these people, but quite simply because I didn't know how to play politics.

It was an art I never mastered.

Being an ass-kisser is a talent many people are born with. I just couldn't get the knack. I envied anyone who could so blatantly, and without a trace of consciousness, accommodate those on a higher rung of the ladder. They were the ones who had better positions and made more money.

I went in the exact opposite direction. I challenged my bosses, or ridiculed them. This was no way to get ahead. I would say things that would get me fired.

Sometimes, however, I didn't get fired. My irreverence would work for me. While still in the early stages of my career, I was hired by Jim Jordan, the legendary New York advertising figure who was famous for such lines as "ring around the collar".

His theme lines left me cold, but he himself, was one of the most dynamic people I've ever known. Jim took a liking to me from the first time I'd met him, which was when I was interviewing for a job.

I got the job of copy chief in the creative department. In a meeting with the agency brass (I have no recollection as to what I, someone relatively unimportant in regards to agency policy, was even doing in the same room with them), Jim produced a letter that had been sent to him by one of the big clients. He proceeded to read it aloud.

"We would like to praise James J. Jordan," the letter began. "James J. Jordan is one of the ablest creative people our company has ever had the pleasure of working with. James J. Jordan gives us special attention at every turn. We are extremely pleased that James J. Jordan is on our team. Thank you, James J. Jordan."

Following this self-congratulatory reading, a lone voice was heard to say, "Signed, James J. Jordan".

In the stunned silence of the room, I wondered

who could have said such a thing. And then realized it was me.

Jim, classy guy that he was, laughed at what I'd said. "I make the jokes around here, kid."

He could have shown me the door to unemployment, but instead he offered me an even better job than the one I already had, that of creative director of the Boston office. Jim had become one of my most supportive allies.

But, alas, my tenure in Boston didn't last. Politics again. I eventually went freelance because freelancers, not being part of a company, are much in the same category as rented furniture.

You are functional. You don't have to be used all the time. Only when there is a need for you. You get the assignment, you do the assignment, and then you vanish. If you are extremely functional (doing good work consistently), you will have the best of both worlds, lots of work with lots of freedom.

The difference between you and someone on staff is that you, as a freelancer, are being paid for your expertise and your opinion.

People on staff may also be hired for their expertise...although not always for their opinions.

As a writer both in the United States and in Europe, I felt more comfortable being freelance. I could be candid, almost to the point of rudeness, and no one would take offense. After all, I was an outsider, not one of them. Therefore my views were those of an outsider, a safe position to be in.

On those occasions when clients made fools of themselves—which was often—I could, if I wished, make that fact known...with impunity.

Such an occasion occurred when I was freelancing in London. One of my main sources of income was a London ad agency owner called Mike Robinson. He was flashy and well connected, but would get rattled when a client became disgruntled or displeased.

Because of his proclivity for panicking, he thought nothing at calling me at all hours of the day and night as he did one particular midnight just as I'd drifted off to sleep.

"Be at Park Lane at seven in the morning," he'd said.

Mike didn't have to identify who or what was on Park Lane. He was referring to the headquarters of his biggest client, Estee Lauder/ UK. They wanted to use an American made TV spot but didn't want the American voice over that went along with it. My job was to find a British one.

"Any particular problem?" I had asked.

"He hates the voice."

"He hates the voice?"

"He hates the voice you chose for the spot."

"You told me to go ahead and choose a voice."

"Maybe I did, but he hates the voice you chose."

"Well, that's no problem. I recorded three others as well."

"And they're on tape?"

"They're on tape."

"Bring them. Seven sharp tomorrow. Don't be late."

I wasn't late. But it felt like I was because the office of the managing director was full of people waiting for me. It was as if their lives depended on what I was bringing them.

The managing director, a jowly, middle-aged man with hair slicked back and in the uniform that most heads of companies in London went in for—blue pin-striped suit from Savile Row, blue shirt with a white collar, big floral print tie, black shoes with gold trimming—was sweating.

His minions were also sweating. Their eyes darted back and forth from their boss to me as if they were watching a tennis match at Wimbledon. From the tension in the room, I could only surmise that they were in a great state of fear.

Mike's manner didn't help matters. He seemed as panicked as the others. He introduced me. "This is Charles, our American. "He's been working on this assignment," he stuttered. "And he's brought more voices for you to consider."

"That's right," I chimed in as I put the cassette of voices into the player. "No need to worry. You're covered. I'll just switch this on, and you can listen for the voice you like."

The first voice came on and I immediately realized I'd made a mistake. I hadn't reversed the tape.

The voice came barreling out of the speaker, "Estee Lauder lips and Estee Lauder Eyes and now Estee Lauder eyelashes..."

I hadn't intended to play that voice, but before I could fast forward, the managing director spoke up.

"That voice! I love that voice! That's the voice I want!" he said excitedly.

I then had to make a decision. My left brain told me: Don't do it, but then my right brain said mischievously: Do it! Go ahead, do it! They went on jabbering a bit. And then I spoke, "That's the voice you said you hated."

Total and complete pandemonium sounded in the room. It felt as if the air had been sucked out of it and everyone was choking to death. The managing director's face took on a bright red hue. His staff wore a collection of quivering facial features. Mike Robinson looked like he was going to keel over.

I had humiliated the managing director to near death. And yet no one could blame me. I was only the messenger of death. I had merely responded to his enthusiastic claim that he loved the voice.

Witnessing the suffering going on in the room, I knew I could square matters with a simple statement.

"Voices sound completely different on tape than they do when actually on the commercial. You can love a voice on tape and hate it on the film."

Whew. Sudden relief. People were breathing again. I had saved the client from drowning, figuratively speaking.

On another occasion, in another city, San Francisco, I actually did save a client from drowning when he fell into San Francisco Bay.

The ad agency I was freelancing for had invited some clients, including a guy named Patrick, out for drinks and dinner on Forbes Island, a short boat ride from Pier 39 in San Francisco.

Patrick was an alcoholic without even the slightest chance of recovery. I never held that against him. What I held against him was that he was also a complete moron. He would never shoot down my best efforts but, instead, would maim them by taking his red pencil to them, adding words, deleting others, rendering them unrecognizable.

The agency that hired me did so because I could usually clean up the mess Patrick was making.

One thing I found was that I could always level with Patrick. I just had to wait until he was really drunk.

"Patrick," I once said to him after one late night months before in New York after a shoot when he'd been boozing and was near-blotto, "You are a horrible, revolting, insignificant piece of shit if I ever saw one.

You should be shot."

"Nahhh ehhh uhhh nahhh nahhh?" was all he could reply,

I knew Patrick would never remember what I was saying, and sure enough, the very next morning, at breakfast, he greeted me with: "Good morning, Charles. I changed a few things in your script…"

So anyway, here we were on Forbes Island which was the smallest island I had ever visited. Years before, someone had had the brilliant idea to scoop out the interior of this island and make it into a restaurant/bar.

When getting off the boat, you would immediately enter the restaurant down a ladder. Once inside, it was quite a remarkable place with mahogany fittings, bar, table, chairs, floor. We had dinner and drinks. Patrick had three drinks to everyone else's one.

Then, on the boat ride going back, I saw him stagger onto the deck and immediately fall overboard. We were close enough to the dock that I could immediately throw him a line and begin to haul him up, but it took a few others to help. We finally got him on the deck and saw that he didn't need any medical attention. He was merely wet. Not that he noticed. All he wanted, demanded, was a drink.

"Nahhhh nanna ehhh nuhhhh…and so on and so forth."

In his incapacitated state, he allowed himself to be walked/carried into a bar that was just a few paces from the dock. There, we propped him up on a stool where he created a Pacific Ocean of his own on the floor below him.

The agency account executives acted as though this was the most normal occurrence in the world. A man dripping wet, propped up on a stool, sucking on one scotch after another.

They weren't going to embarrass or humiliate him by pointing out his condition to him.

When witnessing scenes like this, I would often think of the books written about codependency.

They talk about how destructive it is when company employees cover up for one another and how the quality of work is decreased.

Yet, codependency continues on a grand scale.

When a company covers up for someone incapable, and everyone is doing a little dance around him or her, the entire company suffers and productivity can diminish by 50 percent. As a freelancer, I have watched a number of companies destroy themselves this way.

Whatever happened to Patrick, you may wonder. I have no idea. He is no doubt dead. Maybe he fell off another boat, and someone had the good judgment to just let him drown.

As for me, I remained a freelancer until I quit to write full time. Looking back, I was very fortunate in my bubble of anonymity. It allowed me to work steadily without have to get involved in company politics.

And yet I couldn't help but feel sorry for those crazy, comic, codependent characters all twisted up in the corporate world.

37

Neighbors...and why some people live hundreds of miles from the nearest one.

It's great when you have great neighbors as I currently have. But this wasn't always the case.

I once had a neighbor who took revenge on me every chance he had because of something my six year old son said.

We had recently moved into a house in Chiswick, which is about six miles from Marble Arch in the center of London. While gardening one day, I saw my six year old son, John, standing on a garbage can and pointing to someone in the next yard.

"Look," he screamed. "A witch!!!"

I looked over and saw that the person John was pointing at was the grandmother of that family, and she did, indeed, resemble Margaret Hamilton, the actress who portrayed the witch in "The Wizard of Oz".

For a child to see someone whom he thought could turn him into a frog, this was a shock and I could well understand John's outcry, but I whisked him off the garbage can as fast as I could and told him that he had to be more polite, that she was not a witch, and that well...she only looked like one.

A short while later when John and I were inside, someone rang the doorbell. Ours was a Victorian house with an opaque glass front door. On the other side of it,

I could see the outline of a very large adult.

When I opened the door, I saw it was Jim, the son of the woman John had so disparaged. He was fuming.

"Your son just called my mother a bitch," he said angrily.

"No," I said without thinking first, "a witch".

This little exchange put a damper on any future pleasantries. And there was absolutely no negotiating on another matter that was driving us crazy: Jim's Sunday morning gatherings with his motorcycle gang.

There they would be, the British equivalent of the Hell's Angels, all of them big and brutish-looking, along with their motorcycle hags, as they called themselves, revving up their bikes outside our front door.

Talking to Jim about these weekly disturbances, got me nowhere. "Stuff some cotton in your ear'oles," he would advise me. "Sunday morning is my recreation time…the only time of the week for me to have my mates over. I work the rest of the week, you know. Unlike some geezers I know of…"

His inference was quite clear. It was thought that because I was a freelance writer working out of my home office, that I loafing around all day doing "piss all" as they called it.

No doubt it caused my neighbors a certain amount of envy on those frequent occasions when I would be picked up by stretch limos. These were sent by production companies fetching me to film studios where we were making TV commercials.

When stepping into one of these limos, I could sense Jim's wife, Pam, watching me from an upstairs window. Pam, who was stationed at that window day and night, was the neighborhood crime watch and did, indeed, stop burglaries from occurring.

She also knew everything else that was occurring.

This led to them copying us in the things we bought. If we bought a new car, they did the same. If we bought a new TV, you can be assured there was a delivery of a new TV to them the next day.

We sent our kids to a private school (known as public school in England). They took their kids out of the state school and enrolled them in the same school.

I found their copycat behavior amusing, but not their numerous extremely noisy backyard get-togethers with about 1,000 relatives, many of them arriving by, you guessed it, motorcycle. These food and fun fests would begin in the afternoon and end (if we were lucky) in the early morning hours.

They'd bought a huge inflatable pool, twice the size as the one we'd installed for our kids, and the noise of people splashing about in that gigantic container was deafening, as was the music that blared out of enormous speakers.

These episodes weren't the first I'd had with noisy neighbors. I once lived in an apartment where the person above me seemed to wear hob-nailed boots, even to bed.

When you are contending with that kind of thing, your whole life is affected, morning, noon, evening, and night. You become extremely sensitive to every sound that person up there is apt to make, right down to the flushing of a toilet at three in the morning accompanied by the clomp, clomp, clomp of heavy feet.

It gets to the point that you know their entire schedule. You know when they go to work and you know when they come home. You know if they are gone for the weekend, or worse, if they have people staying for the weekend.

You especially know if they are giving a party. The

whole building trembles due to their insanely loud music.

The fact is, you are living with people you wouldn't, in a million years, choose to live with.

So what can you do to combat the situation? Short of carpeting the ceiling, not much.

Complaining to those creating the disturbance doesn't usually work. If you lose your temper or get crabby with them, they might even take up Morris Dancing at midnight just to show you who's boss.

Complaints to the management of an apartment building results in a gentle note to the offending party living above you, but those don't usually work, either. In fact, the more you complain, the more the management is going to consider you the nuisance.

Perhaps the answer would be to go out a lot, never be home. You could go to the movies and see the same picture over and over again until you are sure your neighbors are in bed.

And then there are the bars where you could drink a lot. That way you could be completely blotto when arriving home.

An extension to the drinking idea is that you could eventually go to AA meetings. There's usually a meeting every night. And that way you might even meet people you like and acquire a lively social life outside of meetings. More to the point, outside your home.

Before you do any of those things, however, apply some psychology. Why do your neighbors make noise in the first place?

You have to recognize that your noisy neighbors, whether they be ones who live next door or above you, don't consider themselves the problem They consider you the problem. After all, it's you who's making all the fuss.

Try seeing things from their perspective. It's time

to take some responsibility for the situation the way it is.

You're the one who called the cops when their July 4th party had carried on way into July 5th.

You're the one they call old prune face behind your back because of the way you look at them whenever your paths cross.

You're the one who makes them scared to even sneeze for fear you'll be lodging another one of your damned complaints.

When you look at it this way, everything changes. How would you like to be in their shoes, knowing that you are under constant surveillance? That there is someone listening for your every sneeze?

For them, it's like having the KJB or the Gestapo living next door.

This is a two-way street, with you probably much more the aggressor than the other party. The truth is, your neighbors are merely living their lives. Living life is noisy.

They are doing what comes naturally while you are not living your life at all because you are afraid of a little disruption.

Hate to tell you this, but should you finally face the facts, maybe you will see the situation as it really is, that you're the one who is creating the dissension, that you're the one who is making their lives hell.

Now what are you going to do to make amends?

38

Being pregnant and having total strangers reaching down and patting your stomach.

Pregnant women, beware. There's no telling when someone will appear out of nowhere, reach down and violate your person with a pat on your tummy.

"My, my," the person with the roving hands might predict, "I think you are going to have triplets!"

What's with these people who think this is okay behavior? It's as if having a baby bump puts you in the category of public domain.

And what about the questions people ask? For example, "How many attempts did it take you to get you pregnant?"

"This was artificial insemination, right? Which one of you has the fertility problem—you or your husband?

"What kind of selfish, unthinking person are you that you would bring a child into a world like this?"

"Let's hope the kid doesn't inherit your nose."

"You have one hell of a nerve. I've been trying to conceive for seventeen years. And there you go and have one right off the bat."

"You look like a sturdy gal who could drop one in the field."

"Either you are grossly overweight or you are pregnant. I can't figure out which."

"Just what the world needs, another mouth to feed."

"If you expect me to get up and give you my seat just because you got yourself pregnant, you can forget it."

"If it's a girl you can always drown it."

"Sorry lady, I don't pick up pregnant women in my taxi."

"Are you freaking crazy?"

"You're the surrogate mother, right?"

Or the supposed joke: "Do you know who the father is?"

People actually say things like that according to the women I have interviewed on this subject. But worse than what they say are the things people do.

"I couldn't believe it," Susan Anderson of Oregon, told me, "there I was at the airport, and they wouldn't let me pass through the gate unless I was patted down by a female security person. They thought maybe I was trying to smuggle a bomb on board."

Another woman I talked to, Marynell Hanley of Florida, told me of a house detective in a department store who followed her from one floor to another. "He probably thought I was stuffing toasters and mattress covers under my sweater."

Jibes, remarks, and tasteless jokes seem to proliferate once a woman starts showing, with men being the main proponents of bad taste.

George Carlin, the comedian, theorized that men can't get over the fact that it was women who created them. It makes them feel that women have the upper hand. And that's goes against the grain. Hence, the practice of the rather unwelcome remark.

This is bizarre behavior. Though maybe not as bizarre as the act of having a baby because, really, what does anyone know about raising a child? The answer to that question is, basically nothing.

When being interviewed on the BBC in London recently, I commented that people tend to spend more time discussing where to have dinner than why to have children, and the host asked me, "Well, why did you have children, Charles?"

"We couldn't think of where to have dinner," was my reply.

I can't recall my wife or myself actually sitting down and discussing the pros and cons of having a child.

Virtually any other achievement in life calls for training of some sort, to become a lawyer, for example, you have to pass the bar exam. To become a doctor means medical school and interning and all the rest of it. Even when applying for a driver's license, you have to take eye, road, and written tests.

When it comes to the most important job on the planet, creating an actual human being, made of flesh and blood, shouldn't people who undertake such an enormous responsibility spend at least some time considering the consequences?

The idea of a tiny, helpless bundle of joy is extremely appealing. But that bundle doesn't remain tiny and helpless forever. Once the child hits puberty, the odds are that you will be stuck with a sullen, depressed, and secretive individual who regards you as one would regard a Martian.

This is where useful training would come in. Parent training should be compulsory in the same way wearing a seat belt in a car is compulsory, for one's own safety. If people choose to go forth with a family expansion plan without the aid of experts, they could be heavily fined, even imprisoned (okay, that may be going a bit too far).

So when a pregnant woman is accosted by someone yelling, "You'll be sorr-ee," from across the street,
she shouldn't take offense, but regard it as a rather
helpful forecast of what the future may bring.

The heckler probably knows from experience.

39

People who make disgusting messes in public places.

Such as public restrooms. How many times have you gone into the gents or ladies room only to find a blizzard of wet toilet paper all over the floor, obscene graffiti on the mirror, the toilet seat wet with someone's urine or worse—evidence of what the person had for dinner—and the toilet not even flushed?

It's as if people consider public restrooms as places to take out their frustrations and to give in to their inner "pigs".

And how about the supermarket parking lot? How many times have you seen a car pull out leaving a dirty diaper in its space?

Okay, while I'm at it, why is it that movie theatres become landfills? Do the people who dispose of their oversized popcorn containers and giant soft drink cups by dumping them on the floor do the same at home? Probably.

Back to restrooms such as the restrooms in certain restaurants. Customers don't even get the chance to be first in filthifying them...they are disgusting to begin with due to management that couldn't care less.

If the restrooms are like this, you have to wonder what the kitchens are like. Okay, don't even go there or you may never eat a meal out again. It's not surprising that restaurant kitchens are strictly off limits to customers. Step one foot inside, and you will be quickly invited out again.

Restaurant kitchens that are in the open and in plain view of customers are supposedly cleaner, although who knows? Have you ever scrutinized one?

But enough about restaurants and onto other places where people make messes, like on trains. One of my special aggravations, the kind of thing that makes me crazy, is the sight of someone putting his or her feet up on seats on a train.

Living in England for a long time, I became "The Guardian of the Seats" on British Rail. My eyes would widen and I would stare at someone who might have his or her feet on a seat until that person got the hint.

But there was one time that could have led to my early demise. I was commuting home from London to Cambridge in the middle of the afternoon and there were only two of us in the car. Looking over, I saw that this yarbo (British slang for thug), had his sizable motorcycle boots up on the seat. He was a large yarbo with tattoos and piercings, and I could almost see him stomping people with those boots.

"Kindly take your feet off the seat," I found myself saying.

The guy turned his head slowly toward me and growled: "What the fuck did you say?"

"I said kindly take your feet off the seat."

"Who the fuck are you?" he inquired.

I could have said that I was an official working for British Rail, but instead replied, "I'm a paying passenger who might, next time I ride this train, be sitting in the seat where your filthy boots are at this moment resting…"

"Well, you can go and fuck yourself, mate."

"Do I have to get the conductor, or are you going to do as you are being asked?

"You're a bloody American, arncha? What the fuck are you doing in my country, telling me what to do?"

"Just that. I'm in your country telling you what to do. Now, please, take your bloody British boots off that seat. It's just a common courtesy so that the next person sitting there doesn't have to get his or her clothes dirty…"

Just then, the train pulled into Stevenage Station, where the yarbo was obviously getting off. Very slowly and deliberately he took his feet off the seat and even more deliberately got up and walked past me, a smile that was more of a grimace painted on his face.

I made believe I was reading, but was, in reality, prepared for him to smash me one before getting off the train. Had he lunged, I was ready to bash him with my book.

Fortunately, he just got off, although violence was probably in the forefront of his so-called brain.

As if this train experience wasn't enough, the very next week, I was traveling up to Edinburgh from London. It was an overnight journey, so I decided to go first class where it wouldn't be noisy.

Settling down in my first class compartment, I was glad to be the only passenger. In a few minutes, I was nodding off, but was groggily aware that someone had entered the compartment and that he had taken a seat.

Gazing out from half-closed eyes, I sized up the person coming in. He had obviously snuck into first class from his second class compartment..

Oh well, I thought, live and let live, and then resumed nodding off, only to be rudely awakened by something the man was doing.

He was standing and urinating on his seat.

"Get out of here, you disgusting pig," I shouted. In a moment, he was gone. I rang for the conductor.

"What is it, sir?" the conductor asked in a thick Scottish brogue.

"You better cordon off the first seat on your right. Some guy was in here urinating on it."

"Accccchhhhhhhh," the conductor said, "He was English!" Satisfied with his own resolution on the matter, certain no Scotsman would have ever done such a thing, he punched my ticket and left the compartment.

I learned later that British Rail seats are treated to withstand any number of liquids, the bodily type or otherwise, that they are absorbed into the fabric. Who knows what else may be hidden in those seats, Jimmy Hoffa, maybe.

As far as the conductor's comment that the urinator was English, it is true historically that hygiene isn't exactly the number one priority of many a Brit. Walking through a crowded department store or riding the underground tells you that.

In America, we are used to central heating and so we take more showers. Very few Americans "pong". But that doesn't stop a number of residents in the USA from trashing not just restrooms, but parks. Ever see what a park looks like after a Sunday crowd? If you collect soft drink cans for a living, this is the place to come.

What else do you find in public parks? Well, there are the needles. And there are the used condoms. There's nothing as dead looking as a dead condom.

The people who create these scenes often look well kempt and fashionable. But don't let appearances fool you. The sloppiest looking person might be the world's top neat freak.

Even your everyday murderer won't just leave a body lying around. He'll place it in a dumpster.

But some of the most elegant gents and ladies think nothing of peeing in public swimming pools.

And otherwise respectable motorists have no problem throwing Macdonald's hamburger packs or Pepsi containers out their car windows.

And exquisitely dressed matrons see nothing wrong with sticking a wad of gum under the table.

And those sweet young things? They would be surprised if you objected to them disposing of their sanitary napkins in public telephone booths.

There are laws, however, that try and curtail the actions of people bent on rendering a place less than pristine. In New York, for instance, there's a law against spitting on the sidewalk although I've never seen anyone hauled into a paddy wagon for doing so.

Additionally, there are signs on the highway threatening thousand dollar fines for littering. But has anyone really ever been fined?

And there's a law in the California Penal Code prohibiting the disposal of a banana peel by throwing it on the ground. I don't remember a banner headline reading: NOTORIOUS BANANA PEEL DISCARDER APPREHENDED!

Maybe we should copy the way things are done in Singapore. Spitting your gum out on the street is punishable by jail time and a fine, and maybe even some whacks with a cane for repeat offenders.

I'm not advocating the cane, although there are times when I feel that would be too lenient.

If you feel sick after reading this piece, well, you're supposed to.

40

Untamed kids and the parents that won't control them.

I'm sitting in a restaurant with a family friend, his young son of five years old, and a few other people. The first thing the child does is to bury his face in the bread basket. I watch as he grinds his head around into the bread rendering it a snotty, salivary mess and totally inedible.

The dad doesn't look like he is going to do anything about it. He just sits there looking adoringly at his little boy.

It's not my policy to correct somebody else's child, but without much warning, even to myself, I do just that when the child starts carving the table with his dinner knife.

Surprising the child as well as myself, my hand involuntarily shoots out as I grab the child's wrist.

"No!" I say loudly enough for the people at the next table to turn around. Like some sort of law enforcement officer, I make the child drop the knife. He is shocked. So am I.

That kid has never heard this word "no" before—that's obvious.

Meanwhile, the dad's facial expression hadn't changed. He still sits there looking adoringly at his little boy.

Far more maddening than this errant child is his parent. If that kid was to set the tablecloth on fire, the dad would probably just continue smiling.

In some quarters, an out of control child will be considered cute.

"Do you know what our little angel did the other day?" a proud parent will beam. "He tried to burn the house down. We had to tell that sweet little rascal that he mustn't play with matches, but we let him keep his supply when he started crying that we were going to take them away..."

These little monsters dictate what goes on in the home. They will eat only certain kind of foods—everything else is dumped on the floor. They will go to sleep only when they are good and ready, not when somebody else, like a parent, is good and ready.

Antisocial behavior isn't just tolerated, it's encouraged by letting the child get away with murder time and again.

Going to school does nothing to quell the child's appetite for mayhem. Should a teacher raise his or her voice or attempt to control the child with physical restraint, an unholy uproar will ensue.

Children know more about the law than you can imagine. They get all sorts of information from watching TV, and they are aware of cases in which teachers are put on trial for what our lawmakers now term "child abuse".

So all the child has to do is tell his mother or father that Miss Jenkins touched his angelic little person—and watch out.

Outrage on the part of the parent will be the order of the day. Threats of suing the school are not unheard of. Schools are terrified of lawsuits.

"I was simply trying to stop Timmy from sticking

a pencil up Johnny's nose," Miss Jenkins will explain to the panel of unsmiling, unsympathetic school officials. But at the same time, she will understand that it's in the school's best interests to do as the parent demand, and that she be fired.

That's the way it is in schools today. Even if a child of seven is smoking pot in the back of the classroom. Some teachers will hesitate to report it as it could reflect upon them in a bad way. There'll be no support from the school. The school recognizes that the parent is the boss, but not as much the boss as the child.

Children also know, from TV, that they can press charges against their parents if the parents as much as threaten to spank them.

"Kid Power" is a force like never before. These small beings are able to manipulate and madden their parents and teachers to get what they want. And what do they want? How about everything?

Should we blame parents? Absolutely. But then, what do parents know about bringing up a kid?

The fact that many parents are so permissive and have absolutely no idea what being a parent is all about, there is some validity to the blame.

The main premise parents fail is in understanding that they are supposed to be role models for their kids. They are supposed to be strong when it comes to setting boundaries. They are supposed to teach the child right from wrong.

This is where the "no" word has the most benefits. Instead of giving the kid everything he or she wants, or letting the kid do whatever he or she wants, there has to be a strong core of censorship coming from mom and dad.

Parents are not meant to be "friends" with their children. Friendly, yes; "friends", no. There is a difference Children already have friends. What they need from their parents is guidance.

During the Great Depression of the 1930s, parents had enough problem putting food on the table, let alone giving their kids toys, clothes, etc.

Those kids grew up to become "The Greatest Generation" as Tom Brokaw termed it.

In subsequent decades, parents have wanted to give their kids what they didn't have. Hence, the dawn of "The Token Child."

The parents of a token child want that child to represent them. They want their friends and families to "oooh" and "ahhh" whenever little Courtney, Ashley, or Morgan come into sight.

So dad works two jobs to provide the designer wardrobes, the latest hi-tech gadgets, the school year abroad, and when the child is old enough to drive, the sports car.

Meanwhile, the child, bored with all this material wealth, wants something more...kicks, thrills. That can only mean one thing, drugs.

Drug use amongst our kids is now at an all-time, excuse the expression, "high".

In the misguided desire to see our kids be happy and fulfilled, we have robbed them of their motivation and the lessons that come from experiencing the consequences of their actions,

We have, without ever having intended to, ushered them through the door to a negative lifestyle.

What can a parent do when the situation has got so out of hand?

How about drawing boundaries? Taking such action will shock your kids, even make them act out more than ever. Their manipulations, which have always worked before, won't work now. They'll try everything,

but if you don't budge, they won't get anywhere.
Start young, and save a family.

41

Hi-tech product manuals nobody can understand.

Including the people who write them.

Either the people who write hi-tech manuals live, sleep, and eat the products they are writing about and know so much about them that they take it for granted that you do, too…

…Or, they haven't a clue what the product is about and are just winging it.

This latter case would apply to me. As a freelance writer, I was on occasion offered hi-tech manuals to write.

I could write about cars, food, fashion, travel, wine, the arts, and a long list of other subjects, but hi-tech? I just couldn't get my mind around it.

The fact was (and still is), I was terrified of anything hi-tech. My first computer sat on my desk, untouched, for five years.

The manuals I wrote made no sense at all, which was perfectly okay, because so many manuals out there make no sense at all.

Even the people who make hi-tech products don't know what's what half the time.

I did, a long time ago, accept an assignment to

write an ad campaign for Honeywell computers. The client wanted a fresh approach. They wanted the language to be in layman's terms so that the average consumer would understand what was being offered.

This was right up my street. I could do layman's terms. That was my forte; explain the hell out of something so even an infant would know what I was talking about. I'd been doing that with consumer and package goods for years.

So this assignment sounded fine. And it was lucrative. In no time at all, I let my imagination have free rein and worked out a couple of campaigns. You always have to present at least three campaigns because you can never show just one.

I had absolutely no idea what the product was about, but proceeded anyway, creating some rather magical advertising.

Everyone at the ad agency I was freelancing for thought the work was spectacular. But then, none of them knew what computers were about, either.

At the presentation, a large group of people from Honeywell listened raptly to what I was presenting. They looked so incredibly involved that I was mentally congratulating myself that I had made this sale. The agency people were beaming. There was no doubt that I was a genius.

But what I was perceiving in terms of the expressions on client faces as approval was, in reality, total bafflement. These people were, in truth, stunned at the outrageous claims I was making about their computers.

The features I was so grandly boasting about hadn't even been invented yet!

I decided to retire from the world of hi-tech after that. Except that I couldn't. The offers came in more than ever for me to write product manuals. In some cases, the manuals were part of a larger assignment I was doing, and in that case, if I wanted my fee, I had to comply.

Let me explain at this juncture that I have always hated writing anything that was dry or boring. I would try to "soup" it up, give it some energy...even though manuals are not required to do that.

Another aspect of a full assignment was the business letter. Dry and boring doesn't even begin to describe these letters. They're the ones big corporations send out that nobody ever reads.

So to "test" my theory that no one ever reads these letters, I decided to experiment with the one I was writing for a bank manager. I ended it with the words: Love and kisses, William K. MacDonald.

To my knowledge, no one ever commented on how I'd signed off for Mr. MacDonald...including Mr. Mac-Donald.

Anyway, there I was, with all those offers to write manuals and nothing else. I couldn't figure it out, until I realized that no self-respecting writer in the great city of San Francisco was willing to take on such a project. And the word had got out that I did this kind of work.

The other factor that came into the picture was that I had children to feed. So I continued on in these torturous assignments.

Until, one day, I was fired for giving the person who'd hired me, a angry, macho, growling kind of client, the finger.

But I hadn't really given him the finger. He only thought I had.

My second wife, the amazing guru, teacher, author, and lecturer, Betty Bethards, had a solution for me when dealing with this difficult person, and that was to give him a "fluff".

What, you may be asking is a "fluff?" This was Betty's very simple method of getting one's energy up. You would raise your right hand, palm upward, from mid-pelvic area to your head, several times in quick succession.

This action would engage your kundalini power which is based in the second chakra, and ignite your energy flow. It works.

If you are down and depressed, try it.

You can also do this for other people. You just raise your cupped hand in their direction and they will get the benefit.

"When your client turns his back on you, bring you hand up quickly and watch his mood change," Betty suggested.

The next day, as I entered the growling client's office, I saw he was standing with his back to me. Perfect opportunity. I brought my hand up quickly, but not quickly enough. He turned and saw me with my hand in the air.

"Hey," he growled, "you're giving me the finger?"

"No," I said, "I was giving you a fluff."

This being San Francisco, I could see from the look on his face that it would have been better if I'd given him the finger.

"You're outta here," he roared, and that was the end of my manual-writing days. I never had another assignment offered me. And I can't say that I was sorry.

But the reality is that we are in the age of hi-tech, and one can't avoid it.

So I, like other consumers, have to rely upon manuals. Even if they make no sense.

42

Finally, the assumption that everybody loves Raymond.

Enough said. Think I'll save this one for the sequel.